W9-BKQ-077

Saint Peter's University Library
Withdrawn

Classroom Skills in English Teaching
A Self-appraisal Framework

Teachers today are being asked to look at their own performance in the classroom and to ask themselves, 'How well am I doing this, and how can I do it better?' This book will enable both experienced and beginning teachers to identify and evaluate their classroom skills, encouraging them to build on good experiences and learn from bad ones. A practical guide to the basic skills of teaching and class management for beginning teachers and teachers in training, it challenges and extends the thinking and practice of all English teachers, stimulating them to reflect critically on their teaching skills.

Colin Peacock concentrates on the processes of classroom teaching rather than on the content of the curriculum, making the book suitable for teaching programmes at all levels. The skills described include goal-setting, the directive, discursive, problem-solving, and the activity modes of teaching, and the skills of explaining and effective questioning. The evaluation and appraisal of classroom practice are also discussed. Each chapter includes a skills checklist and draws on evidence from classroom research, illustrated by examples of good practice and transcripts of lessons.

Of immense practical value, the book will help teachers to become aware of the range and variety of their teaching skills and confident about developing new ones.

The Author

Colin Peacock is Lecturer in Education in the University of Stirling. Previously he taught for twelve years in secondary schools in England.

Classroom Skills
in English Teaching

A Self-appraisal Framework

Colin Peacock

London and New York

First published 1990
by Routledge
11 New Fetter Lane, London EC4P 4EE

Simultaneously published in the USA and Canada
by Routledge
a division of Routledge, Chapman and Hall, Inc.
29 West 35th Street, New York, NY 10001

© 1990 Colin Peacock

Typeset by LaserScript Limited, Mitcham, Surrey
Printed and bound in Great Britain by Mackays of Chatham

All rights reserved. No part of this book may be reprinted or
reproduced or utilized in any form or by any electronic,
mechanical, or other means, now known or hereafter invented,
including photocopying and recording, or in any information
storage or retrieval system, without permission in writing from
the publishers.

British Library Cataloguing in Publication Data

Peacock, Colin
    Classroom Skills in English Teaching : a self-appraisal
    framework.
    1. Educational institutions. Curriculum subjects : English
    language. Teaching
    420'.7
    ISBN 0–415–03633–X. — ISBN 0–415–03643–8 (pbk.)

Library of Congress Cataloging in Publication Data

Peacock, Colin, 1939–
    Classroom skills in English teaching : a self-appraisal
    framework / Colin Peacock.
        p.   cm.
    Includes bibliographical references.
    ISBN 0–415–03633–X. — ISBN 0–415–03634–8 (pbk.)
    1. English language — Study and teaching.
    2. Teachers — Self-rating of. I. Title.
    LB1576.P288   1990   89–39168
    371.1'02—dc20   CIP

Contents

Contents

Appendices

Acknowledgements

In writing this book I am indebted to many people and would like to acknowledge the contributions they have made and express my thanks:

Colleagues and pupils at Eliots Green Grammar School, Northolt, and Redborne School, Ampthill, where I first acquired my own classroom craft knowledge. Colleagues and students in the Department of Education, University of Stirling, especially Professor Arnold Morrison, now Professor Emeritus of Education, with whom I worked on the English curriculum courses (including the microteaching programme), and who established the conceptual framework for the four modes of teaching on which I have drawn.

The teacher-tutors with whom I have collaborated more recently, sharing the planning and teaching of the initial teacher education programme in English: Fiona Breakes, Principal Teacher of English, McLaren High School Callander, and Norma Cousin, Principal Teacher of English, Alloa Academy.

The teachers (and student teachers) of English from schools in the Central Region of Scotland whose classroom work is described and discussed: Fiona Breakes, Norma Cousin, Hayley Croser, Lynn Cunningham, Tony Kildare, David Kinnaird, Brenda Smith, Stephen Wilson.

Colleagues on the Fourth Scottish Central Committee on English (1981-84) where I first gained access to and discussed the guidelines for rules in group discussion (described in chapter three) and the transcript of pupils discussing the ghost story (used in chapter four).

Members of the English Working Group who helped to create the framework for evaluation (used in chapter eight) as part of the work of the Collaborative Project on Teacher Education implemented jointly by the Department of Education, University of Stirling, and the Central Regional Education Department (1979–83).

Members of the secretarial staff of the Department of Education, University of Stirling, for the typing of classroom transcripts and different versions of the main text: Irene Lindsay, Mary Bruce, Meg Carroll, and Dorothy Kelly.

And, finally, my family, Jill, Ellen, and Rachel, for their forbearance while I have been struggling to get the words on to the page.

That said, the arguments developed in the book and the conclusions reached are, of course, my own, and I take full responsibility for them.

Chapter one

Setting realistic goals

What are the qualities that make a good teacher of English a good teacher of English? Does success depend largely on the knowledge and personal qualities you bring to the classroom, or on the professional skills you have (or have not) managed to acquire in the course of your career? If as a teacher you are to be held accountable for the success you achieve in the classroom, what qualities should count as criteria for success in the complex realm of English teaching? And, if after your classroom performance has been appraised and you are found to be wanting in some respect, what will you be able to *do* in order to improve? How will others be able to help?

The present book will direct attention to one of these topics in particular for detailed investigation – the professional classroom skills that the teacher may or may not acquire – but each of the questions asked will also be taken into account in the chapters that follow. Most people will readily accept the importance of the personal qualities you display as a teacher, and the knowledge and understanding you bring to your classroom. But a surprisingly large number of beginning teachers from both primary and secondary schools and from a range of training institutions claim that the one agreed key feature lacking in their own initial training was actually learning about how to teach. However, many seem to accept that classroom expertise is something you can only pick up from observing other teachers at work or by trial and error yourself. It is not, they believe, something that can be systematically taught and learned.

Certainly, one abiding memory I have of my own early days as a classroom teacher of English in a secondary school is the way in which my morale seemed to soar or plummet in response to the experiences of day-to-day teaching. I remember reaching the end of the school day sometimes filled with self-confidence and enthusiasm for the day to come, while on other occasions I was plunged into gloom and foreboding because of the disasters I had lived through. Inevitably, beginning teachers do make mistakes – and learn as a result. Obviously, experienced teachers too go on making different kinds of mistakes and also go on learning as a result. We are all of us learning to teach all our professional lives – or should be.

You learn from the mistakes you make. As a young teacher on my first day in a new school, for instance, I walked into the book store instead of the corridor when I tried to make an impressive exit from the classroom, with all eyes fixed on me. I remember, too, giving complicated oral instructions about how to set about a writing task to a class of 14-year-olds. The resulting silence was broken by a voice saying, 'All right, sir, now tell us what we've got to do.' There was also a lovingly prepared lesson to introduce an extended project which I unthinkingly scheduled for a warm Friday afternoon. As a result of this experience I never planned anything of real importance for a Friday afternoon again.

Obviously you learn from the mistakes you make. You also listen to more experienced colleagues, you read, and you reflect. As your experience grows and you learn on the job, you develop your professional skills and expertise. And a lesson that pleased you in your first year of teaching becomes run-of-the-mill in your fifth. It also gradually becomes easier to be more dispassionate and analytic about your experiences. Part of the problem for me in those early days was trying to remain objective and detached about the actual experience of teaching and the emotional reactions it brought. In a secondary school you are faced daily by a variety of different classes bringing with them distinctive problems and challenges – problems of preparing and marking work, problems of communication, management, and control. To an experienced outsider the lessons that are learned on the job by a novice teacher may appear to be obvious and the difficulties experienced to be coloured by exaggerated emotion. None the less, we should share some fellow feeling with those young teachers who say that their main objective in teaching a particular lesson is simply to get through it and survive till the end.

Part of the problem for a beginning teacher is that your self-esteem is influenced overwhelmingly by your anxieties about classroom control and a need to be accepted by the class. You want your pupils to be happy and enjoy themselves in your classroom, but not at your expense. When things go well, you are convinced that you are making a deep impression on your pupils, possibly providing them with experiences they will cherish for the rest of their lives. On the other hand, when things go badly, you feel that your contribution to the curriculum could be removed along with the subject you are teaching and nobody would notice any difference. When you reflect, though, it is very difficult to know with confidence what impact you are actually making on the classes you teach, and what has been taught and learned, beyond the signals provided by classroom responses, pen-and-paper exercises, tests and examinations.

In my own case, optimism prevailed. I continued to work in a variety of classrooms and gradually built up a repertoire of classroom skills which seemed to work well for me and for my pupils. I thought more about the nature of my subject and how it could best be taught. Then, when I first moved on to my present field of work – the training of teachers – I experienced new and unanticipated problems. When I was called upon to contribute to a range of courses dealing with different aspects of skills in classroom teaching, I found myself to be surprisingly inarticulate. Teaching is something you do; you don't talk about it or describe it. Initially I had taken for granted that I would be able to communicate to future teachers the experience I had gained and the skills I had acquired. In practice, communication itself was not the main stumbling block; the problem related more to an awareness of what was important and needed to be communicated. Although I possessed a large pool of knowledge about teaching, I found it difficult to draw from it, to organise and articulate it. Most of this tacit intuitive knowledge was buried inside my head and surfaced in unpredictable ways when I observed inexperienced teachers making obvious mistakes or I responded to questions in discussion. The problem is a familiar one. You are unable to recognise what you *do* know, and you fail to grasp what your students *need* to know.

How can you make professional or 'craft' knowledge explicit so that it can be organised and communicated to others? For most teachers the process of classroom teaching seems to be a spontaneous intuitive activity. This is not to say that teachers are therefore generally uncritical or unreflecting. It means rather that the lessons learned from self-criticism and reflection tend to be unorganised and to remain unacknowledged. You learn to teach by teaching.

In the midst of all those complex and varied activities we call 'teaching', the successful and experienced teacher is watching, listening and thinking. You make sudden decisions, often unconnected with your original plans, in order to move the lesson along in a particular direction. And as your lesson proceeds, your pupils too are (usually) watching, listening and thinking too. They in their turn may also take sudden decisions, usually unplanned, in order to move the lesson along in directions of their own choosing. A lesson is partly a meeting and partly a conflict of minds. Both parties in the encounter continue to learn from their experiences and develop their expertise.

From the teacher's point of view, classroom teaching still unfortunately remains a lonely business. You close your door, work in your own classroom with a particular group of pupils, and you rarely see anyone else struggling with similar problems for better or worse. Outstanding teachers often seem genuinely surprised when others see videotapes of them at work and enthuse about aspects of their personal or professional skills. They believe themselves to be just 'ordinary' teachers. They assume that most other teachers are working in much the same way with similar degrees of success. On the other hand, there are some teachers who seem to find it difficult to shift their own point of view to enable them to learn from others unless there is a direct connection between their own mode of working and the example viewed. When this second group see filmed examples of other teachers at work, they find the experience hard to accept because 'that's not the way I would do it...'

Most teachers of English have deeply held beliefs and assumptions about the nature of their subject and how it should be taught. They feel strongly about the kinds of relationship that should exist between teacher and taught, and about the way that classes and the classroom should be organised. These beliefs sometimes create a barrier to new understanding and can frustrate change and development. And for teacher-trainers, inspectors and advisers, it is a continuing struggle to avoid seeking to impose on others the idealised model you carry in your own head of how you yourself used to teach at an earlier stage in your career.

The purpose of the present book, then, is not to urge upon the reader the right or best way to teach English. There are already plenty of enthusiasts in the field who perhaps protest too much. There is, I believe, no right or best way. Different teachers will almost certainly have contrasting aims in the way they think about the subject and about what they want their pupils to learn. They will organise and run their classrooms in different ways, establishing different 'climates for learning' and relating to their pupils in different ways. Different approaches carry with them different strengths and weaknesses and require different professional skills.

The book does aim to help inexperienced and beginning teachers to identify the possible range of skills that will be required of them as they grow in self-confidence and gradually build up their professional repertoire. And it sets out to help them to become more aware of the demands made of them while they struggle to teach successfully. In addition, the book aims to challenge, reinforce and extend the thinking and practice of more experienced teachers of English. It is certainly my hope that for these readers the exposition, illustration and discussion that follow will bring new insights and illumination, and will act as an important resource for their appraisal and support of inexperienced or less successful colleagues.

Certainly it is unlikely that teachers starting their careers today will be able to close their classroom doors as resolutely as earlier generations of teachers did. Nor will they be able to continue to teach throughout their professional lives without challenge. All teachers will need to reflect on their aims, methods and achievements, to exchange ideas, and be open to development and change. In fact, all teachers (not just a dedicated minority) will be expected to be 'extended professionals' - confident and articulate about their aims, possessing a varied repertoire of professional skills, and accountable for their pupils' achievements.

Explicit aims and visible success

How you teach – the resources and materials you select, the way you organise your classroom, the climate for learning you establish and the decisions you take as you work with your pupils – will inevitably be influenced by your beliefs and aims as a teacher. This is why there can be no single right or best way to teach. The 'best' way will depend partly on the kind of person you are and partly on what you – the teacher – are trying to achieve.

If, for example, your aim is to develop your pupils' skills in some aspect of spoken English – perhaps in giving clear directions to help a stranger find a particular place – it is inappropriate to adopt a teaching style which is likely to result in the teacher, not the pupils, talking most of the time. In traditional 'up front' teaching when you are working with the whole class, you are likely to talk a great deal yourself and your pupils are likely to have little opportunity to make extended oral contributions. Similarly, if your aim is to develop pupils' initiative and enterprise as self-motivated learners, it is unproductive to adopt a teaching style that is traditionally didactic or directive. In such a context children have little opportunity to show initiative or take risks. On the other hand, if you wish to communicate essential information that has to be grasped by the whole class, it makes good sense for you to take centre stage yourself and to ensure that all attention is focused on you. In other words the 'best' way to teach will depend as much on your purposes and goals as a teacher as on your own personality and values.

It follows, therefore, that you need to make your aims and intentions clear and explicit not only to yourself but also to the classes you teach. Surprisingly this demand is not as simple and straightforward as it may sound. It is comparatively easy (if time-consuming) to list a collection of sham objectives before putting a scheme of classroom work into practice. They are designed to please or satisfy others – visiting inspectors, heads of department, examiners, head teachers. They are stored in filing cabinets as unread reference documents and are rarely tested out against classroom realities. At the other extreme, many English teachers seem content to venture forth on a scheme of work with no clear objectives at all. At best they try to find out at some later stage what individual children may have gained as a result of the classroom experiences that have been provided.

'Genuine' objectives, on the other hand, should be an important and helpful means of expressing what a particular scheme of work is seeking to achieve and of recognising what has actually been accomplished at its conclusion. They provide a statement of intent and give both teachers and pupils a sense of purpose, direction and eventual achievement. In effect you (the teacher) are saying, 'This is the point of what we are about to do. This is what I hope and intend we will achieve as a result of the work we are going to do together.' Explicit goals act as reference points or benchmarks against which eventual outcomes of classroom work can be judged. Final assessment and evaluation should be directly related to initial aims and planning – what has actually been accomplished at the conclusion of a scheme of work should be measured against what you were hoping to achieve at the beginning. Obviously outcomes will sometimes surprise and sometimes depress you, because you often accomplish more or less than you originally intended, but your starting point ought to be a clear statement of your hopes and intentions for the benefit of the whole class.

Most teachers of English do at present have general aims for the teaching of their subject which they are normally very willing to discuss. Often, as in England and Wales, these aims together with associated attainment targets will make up a common curriculum in schools. Clearly, too, teachers do already constantly make judgements in assessing the work their pupils produce – outcomes in a variety of forms that result from purposeful classroom activities. What seems to be lacking at present is an essential intermediate step – the provision of a genuine and accurate statement of what a particular lesson or sequence of lessons is seeking to achieve. Such a statement can be used both while work is in progress and especially after it has been completed, to identify the levels of success that are being and have been accomplished. And the statement works to the advantage of both teacher and pupils – the teacher establishes a clear sense of purpose and direction, and the pupil has a clear idea of what is expected and what has to be done.

The demand is not for the creation of a series of pointless curriculum 'hoops' for children to jump through. Nor is it intended to encourage you, the teacher, to direct your attention only to the most obvious and visible outcomes of a scheme of work that can be quickly and easily identified – the 'surface features' of writing, for example, like spelling or punctuation, at the expense of meaning and style. Sometimes the least tangible objectives are the most important. My plea is not for an emphasis on trivial and obvious details, but for clarity and explicitness. If an aim is important, it should be articulated and shared; if an outcome is worthwhile, both you and your pupils should be able to recognise it when it has been achieved.

For example, most teachers of English will at some point in their careers have read with a class the short story 'Spit Nolan' by Bill Naughton (1961). If so, most will recognise that one important aim will be for pupils to enjoy the experience provided by the text. 'A sense of enjoyment' is not an aim with an obvious, tangible outcome. Certainly, at the end of the reading you can ask the class a direct question, 'Well, did you enjoy that?', which often encourages a variety of responses from pupils (not all of them helpful). Alternatively, you can put the same question to individuals quietly and without fuss once the lesson is over. Or, again, you could set a written exercise to find out what they liked or disliked about the story. But none of these strategies is necessary. You can gauge pupils' sense of enjoyment simply by watching them as you or they read the text. You are aware of facial expressions and the intensity of their involvement. You recognise and value the absorbed silence in the classroom when the class reaches the death of Spit and the stillness that continues after the concluding words of the story have ended. An experienced teacher picks up such cues all the time in the classroom even if such moments of intense and obvious silent emotion are rare. It is not usually necessary to ask whether a text has been enjoyed. The evidence will be there before you, as you and the class read.

What counts as English?

It is not the purpose of the present book to provide you with a detailed discussion of the aims of English teaching. I am much more concerned with its classroom practice. But it is essential to remember that good practice is always underpinned by good theory, even if teachers do not always make explicit the nature of the theories which support them. If you are to be a successful practitioner, you must have a confident grasp of what it is you are trying to achieve. What is the purpose of your subject in the school curriculum? Why should pupils be compelled to study it? Should the subject labelled 'English' be presented to everyone in primary and secondary schools in much the same form regardless of age, ability, and social and regional background? And we are now aware more than ever that beliefs and values about the nature of English teaching are not fixed and immutable. They change from generation to generation and are likely to be influenced by economic and political conditions. The debates about whether or not to teach traditional formal grammar, about whether or not to introduce all children to the great tradition of English literature, about whether or not to insist on 'correct' forms of Standard English wax and wane. What follows therefore is merely a 'structured overview' of the field, a 'map' to help you to plot and organise your own beliefs and assumptions about the teaching of your subject.

First and still foremost, English is accepted as an essential core subject on the curriculum because it is believed to be the main influence in schools in helping children to use language and to communicate effectively. Parents, employers and teachers of other subjects see it as the responsibility of the English teacher to ensure that pupils can read effectively for a range of purposes, can write clearly and accurately in a variety of registers, and can talk and listen effectively in a variety of contexts.

The emphasis on variety of context and purpose is important. Despite the continuing debate about the importance of Standard English, most teachers now seem to accept that there can be no single model of 'correct' written or spoken English. No such model can adequately serve communication in all contexts and for all purposes. Forms of language that are appropriate to one context or purpose will be inappropriate in another. Or, put more obviously, how you speak or write will depend on who you are speaking or writing to (or to whom you are speaking or writing). From an early age virtually all children develop important oral skills and essential knowledge about how to use language outside school and without any help from their teachers. Similarly, most children independently acquire some initial reading and writing skills which they absorb from their immediate environment – street and supermarket signs and television advertising, for example.

It is obviously part of the teacher's responsibility to develop this existing resource further and strengthen it. But clearly, too, you must go further. Other new forms and registers of written and spoken English which are not part of the child's existing intuitive resources need to be acquired. All pupils, no matter what their social or regional origins, need to increase their language repertoire and increase their self-confidence and skill in using varieties of English. They need to be able to use and make sense of different forms of English to help them to communicate in a variety of contexts and for a variety of purposes. As a teacher of English, you need to help your pupils to break free from the constraints of home and family, neighbourhood and peer groups, but without belittling or destroying the essential ties and bonds that help to give all children their sense of identity. This, basically, is the 'language skills' argument.

'Language awareness' is a second distinct but related area. Here the teacher is less concerned with helping pupils to learn how to *use* language effectively than with increasing their understanding and awareness of the nature of language itself, the part it plays in their lives, and how it can be used to influence and persuade others. Obviously such study can include grammar and the analysis of language forms and structures, but much more is involved in the enterprise. As the term 'language awareness' suggests, courses or schemes of work in this

domain seek to make children more sensitive to the nature of language
– its different forms and purposes in varying contexts; how speech and
writing differ; how language can be used to influence or manipulate us.
It aims to make children more alert towards a phenomenon which plays
an essential and powerful role in their lives, but which they use and
interpret in the main intuitively and without reflection. These aims can
obviously be met by creating separate free-standing courses in the
English curriculum. Or it can be argued that the subject is so important
that it should permeate the whole English curriculum at all levels and be
integrated into the normal work of an English class.

The third area is of great importance and covers the teaching of
literature. Teachers of English in both primary and secondary schools
obviously make extensive use of literary texts in their classrooms;
literature is an essential part of the fabric of the subject. Texts now tend
to be chosen not because they offer pupils a model of written excellence,
but for the meanings they convey and the insights and pleasures they
will bring. The work of modern and contemporary writers features more
prominently than the great tradition of English literature and the
accepted canon of literary works. This does not overlook the skills and
achievements of a range of different writers, but the emphasis in the
classroom is more likely to be on reading for enjoyment and the
personal, social, and historical insights that literature can bring. Work
on literary texts is perhaps akin to the work being undertaken in parallel
creative, expressive subjects, such as Art. And in addition to reading and
responding to different texts, children can be active in producing their
own stories, plays and poems. In this context English is viewed as a
more specialised, creative, aesthetic discipline.

The study of literary texts will help children to develop their own
skills as writers, especially when trying to communicate a personal,
expressive message. Unfortunately, though, you cannot assume that the
skills they acquire by writing in this way will develop further to include
overall mastery of the written medium as a whole, demonstrating that
they are also competent in other kinds of writing tasks. It does not seem
to follow that because you can write a successful story or an account of
a personal experience, you will also be able to write effectively in other
ways and for other purposes. Consequently the study of literature
(whatever form the texts take) together with the opportunity for pupils
to write imaginatively and creatively is no longer generally accepted (as
it once was) as an adequate strategy for attempting to overcome the
entire range of children's communication problems.

In the course of the last 20 years the notion of 'text' has developed so
that classroom materials have become more varied and more closely
related to the lives children lead. Apart from the growing emphasis on
texts written by living authors and especially on those written especially

for young people, 'non-print' texts from film, television and radio are increasingly used. And as you move away from the traditional literary text towards the main sources of children's daily information and enjoyment, you clearly move into the interdisciplinary field of media and communication studies.

A final area is the aim of developing a critical social and moral awareness in children. Perhaps this is an aim shared by teachers of many different subjects, and every teacher should accept a responsibility in some sense as a teacher of social and moral education. But many teachers of English feel they have a special claim in this field and argue that it forms an important and essential strand to their work. Moral and social questions are inevitably enmeshed in the study and discussion of literary texts and have therefore long been an accepted part of the subject-matter of English teaching. What is again more recent (since about 1970) is an increasing agreement about exploring social and personal questions for their own sake and as a starting point for related reading and writing activities. What do pupils think, for instance, about animal rights, or the conflicting demands of freedom and responsibility? This opening up of the subject-matter of English teaching is understandable given the increased emphasis on developing pupils' skills in communication – our first defined area of the map. If as a teacher you are seeking to promote effective communication in speech and writing in a variety of contexts and for a variety of purposes, your pupils have to communicate about something. You cannot teach the process of communication without some kind of product. And so, English becomes 'everything' - because 'everything' can be talked and written about. All the class and teacher need is an appropriate subject and the motivation to explore it.

No one claims that a real map provides a photographic image of the scene it represents. In the same way, the 'map' of the traditions and concerns of English teaching that has been offered here is also abstract and idealised, and is divorced from the day-to-day realities of the classroom. Your own thinking and practice will almost certainly be less neatly organised and more pragmatic. In effect, classroom teaching is usually a hybrid mixture of different traditions and is likely to draw on a number of the models that have been identified here. The purpose of the 'map' (or any model of teaching) is to heighten the reader's awareness and to increase understanding. It should help you to 'see' more clearly. If, after reflecting on the overview offered here, you feel that this is an area of your professional expertise that you wish to understand better and explore further, a selected reading list of books published since 1975 is given in Appendix A.

Translating goals into schemes of work

If you are reasonably confident about your aims as a teacher of English and what it is in general terms that you are trying to achieve, how do you set about translating these aims into actual lessons or longer schemes of classroom work? Again, unfortunately, the problem is not straightforward or simply solved, even though most experienced teachers go about the business of planning and teaching their lessons quickly and unselfconsciously. The previous section demonstrated that the English curriculum comprises a complex interweaving of different purposes and traditions that have evolved over a long period of time. Similarly the business of teaching children in a classroom will be influenced by complex and perhaps unacknowledged values and beliefs about your own role as a teacher and about how children learn best.

The internalised set of assumptions about your aims, your classroom role and the nature of children's learning will inevitably influence the kind of subject-matter you select for your classes, the way you organise and manage your classroom, and how you present yourself to and interact with your pupils. This is why sharing a classroom with another colleague can be such a frustrating and unsettling experience. Teachers of English often seem to want to travel from different starting points along diverging paths to similar or different destinations. How much consensus, one wonders, is possible?

In the course of the past 20 years, for example, there has been a retreat from deliberate, positive teaching in many English classrooms. More emphasis has been placed on children learning than on teachers teaching. Situations are created in order to stimulate learning; children's competence in using language is believed to develop and grow as a result of different kinds of encounter in the classroom. As the previous section indicated, these encounters can include personal and social problems and issues, different kinds of literary and non-print texts, as well as interacting with other members of the class. In this process the teacher acts more as facilitator and resource than as a deliberate, directive teacher. In order to promote learning it is almost as if teachers are trying to reproduce in their classrooms an environment which is similar to that encountered in the 'real' world where we know most children learn easily and unselfconsciously – by trial and error, from others, and by using a variety of human and other resources.

An alternative view does not need to accept that schools should be deliberately made as remote from the real world and as artificial as possible. Most people will readily accept that the two worlds experienced by children inside and outside school must be firmly connected; clearly each depends on the other. But this second more traditional view argues that the classroom must inevitably be to some extent an artificial environment. The school day has its predictable rituals and is usually divided up into neat sections; bells ring and pupils move about from room to room; and children are compelled by law to be present. Above all, it is argued, the main purpose of schooling must be to ensure that children acquire in the classroom the essential knowledge and skills that they do not normally learn quickly and easily in the world outside. Accordingly the balance concerning both what is to be learned and how it should be learned moves away from the individual child towards the teacher. In this approach the teacher has a more deliberate and positive role to play. The classroom becomes less child-centred and more teacher-directed.

The notion of balance between these two polarised approaches to teaching and learning is important. For most teachers a continuum probably exists between the two extremes and you move intuitively along it according to the purposes and context of your lesson. Perhaps, too, most teachers can identify a clear point on this continuum which will typify their preferred teaching style – the way they best like to teach. Certainly, effective teaching, whatever form it takes, presupposes some kind of successful outcome – effective learning. And, in its turn, successful learning normally demands a resource of some kind for the learner to draw on. Admittedly, teachers will despairingly joke that they have taught a class all morning and no one has learned anything, but this is not a representation of teaching that will claim much public support or increase professional esteem. In a school there are many resources for children to exploit in acquiring knowledge and developing skills, but the teacher remains the most obvious resource and should be the most important.

Even if you are willing to accept a less child-centred and a more positive instructional role in the classroom, it is important to reflect on the old professional adage that 'teaching' is not the same thing as 'telling'. Being able to take centre stage and explain something clearly to a whole class may be an important professional skill, but it is also essential to accept the importance of possessing a varied repertoire of skills. Even if you wish to present yourself to your classes as a traditional 'up-front' teacher, there are still available to you many different ways to teach. Certainly you can tell and you can explain. But you can also show, question, provoke, and analyse. You can seek to involve pupils in the subject-matter of a lesson and get them to contribute ideas and examples themselves. You can amuse and you can entertain. Traditional teaching can be an active, purposeful and direct process. Equally it can be more subtle and devious.

How then can you best exploit your assumptions about your subject and how it should be taught and learned, and actually create ideas and plans for lessons or for longer schemes of classroom work? If, on the one hand, you adopt an extreme child-centred point of view, you may argue that you should do nothing at all to prepare for or anticipate what will happen in the classroom. You should simply do your best, given the time and resources available to you, to respond in a sensitive and helpful way to the problems, questions and experiences that your children bring to you. On the other hand, more realistically, most teachers of English are engaged in the daily business of selecting and preparing different kinds of activities and materials for their classes. If this is the case, what procedures should you follow?

Again, in order to simplify and clarify, it is helpful to think about approaching your task in one of two distinct and contrasted ways. One approach is holistic; the other is analytic. The first – holistic – entails starting from an overall theme or topic and moving towards greater detailed understanding and competence in specific parts. The second – analytic – involves starting with details and specifics and moving towards gradually widening understanding and increasingly generalised competence in the use of the skills you learn. Each approach has its strengths and weaknesses, its supporters and detractors; both are affected by changing social beliefs and fashions. And it is a foolhardy teacher who asserts that one approach is better or more effective than the other. However, it can almost certainly be claimed that some teachers are happier and probably teach more effectively using one of the approaches rather than the other, and equally that some pupils are happier and learn more effectively as a result of receiving or experiencing one approach rather than the other. Probably, though, the most important variable in judging success is not the approach itself, but the skills and the commitment of the teacher who is using it.

Most readers will be familiar with the analytic approach to the teaching of English and will have experienced it at some point in their own educational careers. It is the traditional structured approach to teaching the subject. 'English' is divided up into separate parts and each lesson is devoted to a particular aspect of the subject. For example, Monday is language study or grammar; Tuesday is poetry; Wednesday drama; Thursday writing; and on Friday (probably in the afternoon) you read the class novel. It is the mode of organisation that I experienced as a pupil myself and which was still prevalent when I started my teaching career. Under these general headings you can set out a detailed programme of work with clear goals and outcomes. The arrangement is tidy and convenient for both teachers and pupils. It is easy to organise and manage. Everyone knows where they are going and where they have been.

Unfortunately the main drawback to the approach is that the different parts of the subject seem to refuse to cohere; they tend to be experienced by pupils as a series of disjointed fragments. As you try to move upwards from these separate strands of grammar, literature, writing and so on towards the 'top', where the sum of the parts should begin to come together and make sense, it becomes more and more difficult for the teacher to make the essential, appropriate connections between the different elements of the course. What has been learned seems to make little overall sense to pupils and they find it difficult to apply their knowledge to genuine problems. The gap between the world of the classroom and the real world outside seems too great and the work undertaken lacks credibility and 'relevance' to the pupils. When the approach is adopted, teaching can quickly and easily become 'assessment-led'. That is, the teacher organises a menu of assessable outcomes and simply teaches a programme of lessons derived from it, without giving much thought to what sense the outcomes make to the learners involved. If an external authority demands, for example, that children should be able to 'spell correctly frequent polysyllabic words which observe common patterns' (Department of Education and Science 1988: 50), you can simply teach towards that assessment objective without attempting to place the words in context or considering the meanings they convey.

At present, then, until a more acceptable and coherent version can be developed, this traditional analytic approach does appear to contain more weaknesses than strengths and as a result it lacks committed supporters. Current recommended practice encourages instead a more holistic approach to planning. English as a classroom subject is thought of as a unity with all of its constituent parts being connected and interdependent. We murder, it seems, in order to dissect.

When this second approach is adopted, then, classroom work is likely to be organised not in single lessons, but in units or schemes, with each scheme lasting as long as perhaps half a term. Subject-matter is arranged either thematically – 'The Supernatural', or 'Advertising' for example – or is developed from the shared experience of some kind of literary or non-print text. The theme or text represents the 'whole' experience and different kinds of classroom activity and assignment will grow out from it in different ways. With this approach the teacher constantly seeks to make connections between the different elements and to help pupils to construct their own meanings and interpretations. Classroom activities are likely to involve pupils using all four language modes – reading, writing, speaking and listening – and variety and choice will be included in the menu offered to pupils in order to stimulate interest and encourage positive motivation. Whereas in the traditional analytic model of planning the teacher retains a high degree of control over subject-matter and how it is sequenced and paced, with this alternative holistic model there is likely to be a much greater element of pupil control over which tasks are tackled and completed and a greater degree of 'self-pacing'.

Although there are likely to be common central experiences shared by the whole class, there will also be parallel branching tasks which are directed towards different interests and different levels of ability and achievement.

A practical example of the holistic model would be a scheme of work for older secondary pupils jointly planned by a group of teachers using the novel *Kes* by Barry Hines (1968) as its central focus of interest. At its heart was the reading and discussion of the novel itself accompanied by a viewing of the film of the same name. This common experience then led on to the exploration of a range of related topics – the nature of school as experienced by many unsuccessful pupils, family relationships, starting work (or failing to start), hobbies, birds of prey. These topics in their turn involved further reading, writing, and discussion, and the use of a variety of printed resources. Implementing the project formed the total diet of English for a particular class for a number of weeks.

The approach has clear strengths. Classroom work makes sense and can be related to the concerns of the real world. Interest and motivation can be maintained at a high level and pupils often produce work of high quality. However, the approach does also create important difficulties for teachers to overcome. The planning and preparation of a major project demands not only imagination on the teacher's part, but considerable time and hard work in searching for materials and devising a range of tasks. Putting it into practice in the classroom also requires considerable expertise in the organisation and management of pupils and resources. Once the programme starts to branch, there are many activities in progress at the same time for you to keep track of. And perhaps most important of all, the assessment of individual achievement and progress becomes either exhaustingly complicated and burdensome or unsatisfactorily vague.

In the earlier traditional model, a class can be marched down a single road, almost in lock-step, with a clear identifiable outcome to a single common task. Here, pupils are instead engaged in a variety of self-selected activities, working at their own pace. The teacher has to monitor progress and evaluate the different outcomes. Whereas there is a danger that the earlier traditional approach becomes 'assessment-led', here there is the accompanying danger that the approach becomes 'assessment-confused'. For when you offer such a diverse menu of activities for pupils, it is clearly unrealistic and impractical to try to predict at the outset what the goals and purposes of each element in the project are likely to be for each individual child. From the teacher's point of view, it is easier simply to wait and see what turns up in the way of results and to respond in what seems to be an appropriate way. You cope as best you can. Similarly, from the pupil's point of view, with so much choice on offer, it is tempting to select from the menu only those tasks which already interest you and to accept only those demands with which you know you can already cope. There is little encouragement to try to tackle material which presents new challenges or helps you to acquire new skills. Certainly, everyone is kept busy and interested and a great deal may be learned incidentally in the process. But at the conclusion of the project both teacher and each individual pupil ought to be able to recognise with some confidence what has been learned and achieved, beyond the creation of a folder bursting with paper annotated by the teacher's general comments and grades.

Elsewhere I have presented a more detailed case arguing the need for more explicit guidance to be offered to pupils when teachers are planning extended schemes of classroom work and the importance of an initial clear statement of the goals to be achieved (Peacock 1986: chapter 5).

Conclusion

To sum up, then, this introductory chapter has attempted to set the examination of classroom teaching skills in the wider context of the aims and purposes of English teaching. It has considered the difficulties teachers appear to experience in making explicit to others their aims and the intuitive craft knowledge they accumulate in the course of their work. And it has shown how teachers' beliefs and assumptions about the nature of teaching and learning are likely to influence the kinds of lessons they plan and teach.

If you, the reader, are at the start of your career, it is understandable that you will be anxious to gain as much classroom experience as possible and to learn as much as you can 'on the job'. You may be impatient with theory. None the less, as you accumulate essential classroom experience, you should not lose sight of the importance of the values, beliefs and theories that form the foundation of your growing expertise as a teacher. All good practice is underpinned by good theory. Skills are never context- or value-free; they presuppose and depend on what you are trying to achieve.

If, on the other hand, you are already an experienced teacher of English wishing to evaluate your classroom performance and develop it further, the chapter has attempted to challenge your present thinking about your subject and how you set about teaching it. I have argued that unless you are willing (and able) to make explicit what it is you are trying to achieve in your classroom, you will find it difficult either to monitor satisfactorily your pupils' progress or to evaluate your own effectiveness as a teacher.

The chapters that follow will focus attention on the classroom skills you need to possess if you are to teach English successfully and effectively, starting with an examination in chapter two of four distinct ways in which you can organise and manage your classroom teaching. These four approaches are then described, illustrated and discussed as the four modes of teaching.

Chapter two

Modes of teaching – the directive mode

There is, then, no right or best way to teach English. Different classroom approaches have different strengths and weaknesses, different advantages and disadvantages for both teacher and pupils; they create different problems and make different demands. As the last chapter made clear, how you choose to teach will depend partly on your own values, beliefs and personality, and partly on your aims and purposes in planning a particular scheme of work. And you are likely to vary your approach in accordance with the context in which you are working, responding differently to classes of varying ages, attitudes, and perceived abilities.

The present chapter accepts the fundamental importance of a teacher possessing a repertoire of professional skills. If your professional range is not to be limited, you need to be able to draw on a variety of approaches in the classroom and be able to use each confidently and well. You will almost certainly develop an individual preferred teaching style, which will come to be salient in your classroom work and which pupils will recognise as characteristic of you, but this preferred approach should not become the single dominating feature of your teaching. If it does, the extent of your success as a teacher will be qualified and your pupils' progress and achievements are likely to be diminished.

When thinking about different classroom teaching methods, it is possible to distinguish four distinct and contrasted approaches. These four 'modes of teaching' have different characteristic features and require different kinds of professional skill if they are to be used successfully. The terms adopted for describing the different approaches and the number chosen are not universally accepted nor are they claimed as authoritative. Different theorists use alternative terminology and it is possible to construct different models and to think about the practice of teaching in different ways. However, the terms that will be used and the number of modes that have been selected have proved to be straight-forward, practical and helpful in discussions with both beginning and experienced teachers. And they are preferable to the simple identification of a form of classroom organisation, like 'whole class teaching' or 'group work', because they emphasise the teacher's purposes and intentions in adopting a particular approach to classroom work. The four modes are:

(i) traditional directive or expository teaching when the teacher normally works with the whole class;
(ii) a discursive approach which encourages discussion between pupils normally in pairs or small groups;
(iii) an inquiry or problem-solving approach where a high level of responsibility is devolved to pupils to find out for themselves;
(iv) an approach exploiting pupil activity and involving some degree of physical movement, improvisation or role play.

In the chapters that follow the characteristics of each of these four modes, together with appropriate classroom examples for discussion, will be examined in turn. The distinctive features of each mode and the demands it makes on both teacher and pupils will deliberately be accentuated in order to compare and contrast their different purposes and likely outcomes. In the reality of the classroom, though, the differences are again likely to become less distinct. Under normal working conditions you will find the modes begin to merge and blur. Within a single extended lesson, for example, an experienced teacher is likely to move from one phase to another, successfully exploiting different approaches and not always sure how a sequence of activities should be categorised.

The characteristics of the directive mode

Traditional 'up front' whole class teaching still appears to be the most common and most popular way for teachers to teach. In the words of a young teacher starting his career, it seems to be 'the natural way to teach'. In fact many experienced teachers appear to feel uneasy or even guilty if they do not act out their traditional role in the limelight, working with the whole class and probably burning up quantities of nervous energy. They believe that is the right and best way for teachers to earn their living. Virtually everyone has experienced this mode of teaching as a pupil and it carries with it the hallmark of many years of professional experience. It is thought to be 'tried and tested'.

For example, a typical English lesson implemented in this mode would involve a text of some kind. The teacher would set the scene for the lesson with an oral introduction related to the text and connections would possibly be made with the content of previous lessons. The text would then be read (either aloud by the teacher, or by a series of pupils, or silently by the class). There would then follow a sequence of questions led by the teacher and focused on features of the text or issues connected with it. Not everyone in the class would participate. Individual pupils would volunteer answers or a question would be directed to someone by the teacher. Finally some kind of written task would be set either directly related to the text that has been read and 'discussed' or using it as a springboard for other activities. Work that has been started is often completed next lesson or for homework.

The directive mode is characterised by firm teacher control. As teacher, you choose and plan the subject-matter of the lesson. You work with the whole class as though it were one homogeneous group and you determine the pace and development of events yourself. In the course of the lesson you will almost certainly do most of the legitimate talking yourself. On average, if you audio-record and later analyse a lesson in this mode, you will probably find that you, the teacher, have been talking for about two-thirds of the available time (Dunkin and Biddle 1974: 54 and 137). In contrast, in the classroom itself, when the lesson is actually in progress, you will almost certainly be much less aware of the extent and dominance of your oral contribution.

The pupils, on the other hand, are expected to be more passive. Their attention is focused on the topic selected by the teacher and normally they work as individuals on a common activity. They are expected to listen carefully to the teacher and, when appropriate, to respond to questions. The classroom is usually arranged like a traditional theatre. There is no longer a raised dais for the main performer, but the teacher takes centre stage with the seating laid out so that pupils miss no part of the performance. The sequence of events is usually easy to predict and there are clear cues to the pupils about how and when they can participate in events.

The approach that has been outlined will be familiar. And it is easy to parody and to create its stereotypes. But this mode of teaching is still much used and is popular with many teachers, perhaps with pupils too, and almost certainly with many parents. The tradition that lies behind it is strong. Its roots lie deep in the early elementary and secondary school and beyond (including the church pulpit). To the hard-pressed teacher, the attractions of the mode are still considerable, especially if you are constrained by an external syllabus and have deadlines to meet. You move the class along at your pace and normally in the direction you choose to go. The nature of most school buildings and particularly the classroom 'box' in which you have to work also encourages the transmission of information from teacher to pupils in this directive way. From the teacher's point of view, too, there are the satisfactions that a performance to a captive audience can bring – the pleasure experienced at the end of a lively lesson with a good class. You can enjoy the relationship with your audience in the classroom and thrive on the interaction that takes place between you. And, perhaps most important of all, in the hands of a skilled practitioner the process of teaching is kept as simple as possible. Planning, classroom management, and assessment are all kept relatively straightforward and easy to handle when the mode is used with confidence and skill.

In fact, when you reflect on this mode of teaching, it is not necessary to be negative and dismissive at all. Directive teachers do not all conform to the stereotyped tyrannical lion-tamer or grinding bore. Most readers will almost certainly recognise at least one outstanding directive teacher from their experiences as pupils and still count themselves as being very fortunate to have been taught by the individual in question.

If, as a teacher yourself, you are still using only this mode of teaching in your classroom, your work will certainly be limited professionally and your pupils will be denied a range of important experiences. But, equally, do not underestimate the importance of the mode. It is still likely to be an important part of your professional repertoire. Even if your teaching style is dominated by other modes, you will need on occasions to be directive, perhaps at the start and conclusion of a lesson, perhaps for a longer period of time. And when this is so, it is essential for you to be both confident and effective in your use of it.

The skills of directive teaching

To be an effective directive teacher you need above all to have confidence and faith in yourself, to believe that the activities you have designed for a class are important and worthwhile. For some teachers, even at the beginning of their careers, self-confidence seems to come quickly and easily, but for others it is something that has to be built up gradually over a period of time and it has to be reinforced by a sense of success and approval. Obviously, too, you need to be able to communicate your self-confidence (or at least convey an impression of it) to your classes by your 'presence' in the classroom. You have to be noticed and perhaps appear larger than life to your pupils. You have to accept and probably enjoy being the focus of attention.

These positive qualities are conveyed by the way you move and the position you take up in front of the class and the ways in which you use your face (especially your eyes) and your voice. This is not to say that you need continually to shout, or move restlessly about the classroom, or be exaggerated in manner in order to hold your audience's attention. As we all readily recognise, some very successful directive teachers are characterised by understatement and a sense of calm; their classrooms can be marvellously still, tranquil places. In short, you need to be not 'authoritarian', but 'authoritative', and children need to recognise and accept your authority.

SAINT PETER'S COLLEGE LIBRARY
JERSEY CITY, NEW JERSEY 07306

21

Not surprisingly, then, there are different personal styles associated with directive teaching. It is a classification which accepts many different interpretations. You can be a good-humoured, popular 'entertainer' carrying a class along with you, or you can be a respected, if humourless, martinet driving your class forward ('I hate Mr X, *but* he's a good teacher'). However, no matter what style you choose to adopt in the way you 'direct' your classes, you need to convey to them this sense of authority. Pupils need to feel that you are confident with the subject-matter and purposes of the lesson, self-assured when talking to and dealing with them, and efficient in organising the routines of the classroom. Children seem to be able to intuitively recognise lack of confidence and purpose in a teacher and will chip away at that teacher's authority with skill and often with relish.

Of almost equal importance to this sense of self-confidence and authority is establishing and accepting appropriate rules in the classroom. An accepted system of rules is obviously essential to success in any mode of teaching, but, in the case of traditional directive teaching, rules probably need to be more clear-cut and explicit than in other approaches. One of the strengths of successful directive teaching is that pupils know what is expected of them and how they are to behave. For example, pupils do not normally move about the classroom without permission or speak openly without encouragement (traditionally you have to put up your hand and wait). They also recognise that there are appropriate times or signals which permit movement (to get a new sheet of paper, for instance) or quiet conversation (when working on a task). There are also usually firm deadlines to work towards ('This work will have to be finished and handed in by ...') and clear tasks to be completed. Effective teachers make their rules explicit when they first meet a class and reinforce the rules frequently for as long as their relationship with the class continues.

Classroom rules for the directive mode are long-established and well recognised. But it does not follow, of course, that pupils are ready or willing to accept them. In unsuccessful directive lessons pupils do frequently challenge the authority of the teacher, they manage to divert the planned course of a lesson, often creating considerable noise in the process and failing to meet any deadlines the teacher has set. It is predictable that young people, especially those in their teens, will resent and challenge the authority of the teacher and will seek to undermine the rules that are imposed in directive teaching. No matter how much teachers try to make the content of their lessons interesting and relevant to their pupils' lives, if you are a pupil sitting in the classroom there may be little sense of satisfaction or intrinsic motivation. You are in the class because you have to be there. You are following a course designed and controlled by someone else, and you are required to participate in the activities prescribed. If you are prepared to play the game according to the established rules, there may be personal benefits for you in terms of the knowledge and skills you gain and the additional satisfaction of extrinsic rewards – praise and encouragement from the teacher and eventual success in terms of grades, examination passes and employment prospects. If, on the other hand, you do not experience this encouragement and sense of satisfaction, you may well decide to withdraw your co-operation, and as a result conflict and confrontation ensue.

One important reason for the weakening of the popularity of this mode of teaching in many secondary schools may well be purely pragmatic – the loss of the traditional 'working consensus' between teacher and taught. A sizeable section of the older school population now seems unwilling to accept the conventions that are essential to the effective functioning of traditional directive teaching. Perhaps, too, a large proportion of our children have always found it difficult to learn in this way for an extended period of time. At first the directive mode may appear to be the 'natural' way to teach, but it is not necessarily the natural way to learn. Traditional respect for the teacher has diminished, sanctions now available to schools are more time-consuming and cumbersome to apply, and children are less willing to accept silent passivity and unquestioning co-operation than may once have been the case.

Yet the mode does persist. If you wish to exploit its strengths (as almost certainly at some point in the school day you will), what qualities must you possess beyond those already identified – that is, a sense of confidence and authority in the way you present yourself to your classes, and being able to establish and apply a system of classroom rules? In seeking to answer the question, you will need to explore three further related areas: (i) the importance of the teacher's own perceptual awareness; (ii) the importance of gaining and holding pupils' interest in the content and development of your lesson; and (iii) the importance of effective communication in the classroom (to be dealt with in detail in chapter six). We consider first, then, perceptual awareness in the classroom.

An effective teacher is alert all the time, picking up a wide variety of cues, anticipating events, and ready to take quick action. 'Tunnel vision' in teaching, especially in directive teaching, is a disastrous handicap. Once children realise that you have failed to notice a subtle but deliberate challenge to your authority (as opposed to overlooking one example for good pragmatic reasons), they quickly sense that they are gaining control and you are losing it. You need to remain constantly alert and sensitive to your audience. Skilled practitioners listen and watch, giving their attention not only to the immediate focus of the lesson, but to a wide variety of simultaneous parallel events. They are sensitive to obvious signals, like restless movements, noises and half-heard comments. But they are alert also to less obvious cues, seeking to interpret, for example, the significance of facial expressions ('Are they bored?'), the meaning of a glance from pupil to pupil, or someone intently and quietly writing. As you pick up these signals, construct hypotheses, and seek to interpret their significance, you are likely to take abrupt decisions. You move the lesson along quickly to its next phase, you miss out a paragraph from a reading, you change the direction of the lesson. You may call a particular child to order before he creates more trouble and disrupts the lesson; you repeat instructions or direct a question to a particular child to regain her attention. Throughout the lesson you are monitoring the behaviour of the class and taking decisions in the light of what you have perceived.

The decisions you take must be supported by an ability to handle the routine business of a lesson with confidence and skill. Research has alerted us to the importance of certain 'flashpoints' in the progress of a lesson when problems can quickly escalate for the inexperienced or unsuccessful teacher (Wragg 1984: 44). These moments of high risk are particularly associated with the beginnings and ends of lessons when teachers are trying to establish or regain their authority, endeavouring to get a lesson under way or bring it to a conclusion. And transitions from one phase of a lesson to another can also create special difficulties. For example, you may wish to move from the end of a question-and-answer session with the whole class to a new phase which will involve the setting of a connected writing task. Transitions like these are often complex and difficult to manage. Apart from the possible change in subject-matter and task, you have to explain clearly the nature of the new work, deal with pupils' questions and with mid-lesson restlessness, and perhaps organise the giving out of books and materials, all within a short space of time. Making sure that your lesson flows smoothly and that you can handle lesson routines in an efficient and business-like way are obviously important qualities in any mode of teaching. But it is especially important in directive teaching because you are more isolated and vulnerable when using this mode.

Skills in presenting your lesson (our second main area) and in 'selling' what you have to offer in order to maintain pupils' interest and motivation are also complex. An important dimension that it is only possible to touch on here is the selection of suitable subject-matter and materials – getting the interest and difficulty level right for a particular age-group or class. You obviously have to be able to select themes and texts that will be interesting to your pupils and appropriate to their abilities, and which they will recognise as being worthwhile. This is probably best achieved by trial and error and with help from colleagues.

As you gain classroom experience, you will gradually build up a resource bank of ideas and materials that have been tested out in the classroom and have worked successfully with different classes. These ideas and materials are partly derived from commercially available texts, and partly created from your own ingenuity in scanning newspapers, periodicals and any other sources of inspiration for classroom work. Often, too, resources will be shared within a department and created collectively. (Further reading in this field is suggested in appendix A, 'Resources'.)

Once you have selected or created successful ideas and materials for a lesson, 'salesmanship' becomes largely a matter of classroom presentation. Here the main objective is for you simply to hold pupils' interest and attention. Children are often exceptionally patient and tolerant, but to subject them to long stretches of uninterrupted listening, with occasional opportunities to answer a question or write a sentence or two, taxes their patience unreasonably. At best you should count on an extended concentration span of about ten minutes.

In order to maintain interest, you can deliberately build variation into a lesson plan. You can ensure that events are organised in such a way that pupils will have the opportunity to engage in different kinds of activity at different points in the lesson (perhaps moving the lesson on from the directive mode into another mode of teaching). Such variety is especially important for long units of time when you are with a class for an hour or possibly longer. Above all, you should avoid the lengthy transmission of information to a passive class. Pupils need to be involved actively in any lesson and this includes traditional lessons in the directive mode. When you ask questions orally, you should try to ensure a wide variety of individuals answer; you should respond to what children say and try to relate their contributions to what has already been said or taken place, and you can make use of what they say to develop the lesson further. (See chapter seven for a more detailed discussion of questioning.) No matter how well you personally read aloud, you can ask individual children to read a part of a text aloud to the class (from a book or worksheet, blackboard, or screen); you can also ask the whole class to read a text themselves silently. If pupils have been well 'primed' by explanation, questions and discussion before a reading task is set, even the less successful readers will be able to tackle it and make some progress.

If pupils feel they are being involved in a lesson and are participating in it in different ways, they will be more likely to accept the pace and direction dictated by the teacher. Although the teacher remains firmly in control of the lesson's development, the processes involved are more subtle and self-effacing. And, as a result, you are more likely to avoid hostility and confrontation.

It is also important to try to make your own classroom performance as varied as possible in order to hold pupils' interest and attention. For example, there needs to be variety in the way you use your voice when you are speaking to the whole class – a range from soft to loud, slow to fast, with variety in emphasis, pitch and intonation. You must do your utmost to avoid the criticism levelled against one teacher by a senior pupil in a secondary school – 'He's got a lovely voice to go to sleep to.' You also need to try to use your face expressively and achieve eye-contact with individual pupils. Movement and gesture can also be helpful if they convey a sense of interest and enthusiasm or reinforce important points. On the other hand, you need to be alert to possible problems in the way you behave. If one of your characteristics becomes distracting (a recurring gesture, for instance), or a focus for amusement (the number of times you use a favourite word), they obviously become a source of distraction. I myself remember a teacher who constantly contrasted 'the abstract' with 'the concrete' in his lessons. As a result, a boy brought a piece of concrete to school; it was affectionately named 'The Abstract' and was passed surreptitiously from pupil to pupil during his lessons.

It can help pupils, too, if you deliberately attempt to vary the 'sensory focus' of a lesson or 'vary the stimulus'. You can do this by ensuring that one sensory focus alone does not dominate your lesson. Instead of devoting a large span of time, for example, to listening to an audio-recording of a play, you should try to arrange experiences so that pupils progress from (for example) watching and listening to the teacher, to reading from a text of some kind, to talking and listening to each other, to watching a screen or blackboard, and so on. Variety helps to keep pupils involved and alert.

All these skills, relating to self-presentation, use of voice, movement and gesture, must obviously be used naturally and unselfconsciously. You have to draw on and possibly emphasise the personal qualities you already possess and the behaviour that comes to you easily and intuitively. That said, it is important to remember that, as a teacher, you are certainly adopting a special kind of role in the classroom, and most pupils have firm expectations of the people who take on that role. Do not deceive yourself by claiming that you wish to be 'yourself' in the classroom. A classroom is an unusual context for human relationships; it has its own conventions and traditions. If you attempt to deal with children and gain their co-operation in much the same way as you would when interacting with your own circle of friends or with unknown adults, you are more likely to make your pupils confused and suspicious than to reassure them. In their eyes you will not be behaving like a 'real teacher'. They will expect you to be formal and at least a little remote.

The inter-personal skills you have exploited successfully in the past, in getting on with people and attempting to get things done, will almost certainly fail you in the classroom in your role as a directive teacher – and probably in other modes of teaching too.

Case study: 'Welsh Incident'

The directive mode of teaching can be illustrated by a lesson taught by an experienced teacher with a mixed-ability class of 12-year-old boys and girls in an urban comprehensive school. The class contains a wide range of abilities and levels of achievement and includes children from varied social backgrounds. Desks are arranged traditionally in pairs, facing toward the teacher's desk and the blackboard.

The context of the lesson is a unit of work derived from material in an English course book and developed further from what is presented there. This unit of work – 'Escape from Kraznir' (Seely 1982: Book 1, 145–56) – was spread over a number of weeks and exploits the children's interest in fantasy and magic. It involves the planning of a successful escape from the fictitious Castle Krill in the hostile land of Kraznir. The escape team is carrying secret war plans and has to make its journey through the dangers of river, desert and forest back to the threatened homeland of Slinsil. The teacher's planned scheme of work concentrates on the unfolding of this escape narrative but also includes additional lessons which branch out into a number of topics related to the escape. These additional lessons include researching the lay-out of real castles close to the school, as a background context to the imaginary Castle Krill, and short literary texts to help create an imaginative context for the adventure.

The particular lesson to be described and discussed involves a close reading of Robert Graves's poem 'Welsh Incident' (Graves 1959). The poem takes the form of a conversation between two unnamed individuals – a main story-teller and an active, inquiring listener. The narrative is a 'tall story' about the strange creatures ('All sorts of queer things, things never seen or heard or written about') that came crawling out of the sea-caves at Criccieth to be greeted by a large gathering of local townsfolk led by the mayor. The classroom reading of the poem, and the task and questions that follow it, were connected to the Kraznir project by the description of the strange creatures. In the poem readers are encouraged to use their imaginations to picture what the creatures looked like and how they behaved. After the lesson, pupils were to go on to write their own accounts of being attacked by strange creatures of their own devising in the course of their flight from Castle Krill.

The lesson is organised in three phases:

(i) a brief introduction; the teacher reads the poem aloud; initial explanation to the whole class about the poem's structure; a second reading aloud by two pupils;

(ii) a note-taking task focused on the subject-matter of the poem; initial teacher-led questions to the whole class to monitor pupils' progress;

(iii) an extended teacher-led question and answer phase with the whole class (derived from the task and developing it further); summary and conclusion.

The development of the lesson is now described in more detail with selected illustration and discussion. When a lesson transcript is given, comments concerning the decisions taken by the teacher and the skills she displays are added in parentheses.

The lesson begins firmly and confidently, with the teacher indicating that the poem in question is to be read and ensuring that all pupils are ready and prepared for the reading:

Teacher: ...there's a poem there called 'Welsh Incident'... 'Welsh Incident'. Just turn straight to page eleven. Never mind looking through the pictures just now. Page eleven. Right, Lawrence?... 'Welsh Incident'. I'm going to read it through and then I'm going to get two people to read it through because it's really a poem for different voices.... Okay... Scott, have you found page eleven?

Pupil [Scott]: Aye.

Teacher: Well, just sit with it, eh? There's one book between two... right.

She ensures that the class has settled and everyone's attention is directed to the text. Then she begins to read the poem aloud herself. As in the introductory phase, when she is preparing the class for the reading, her voice is loud and clearly audible; the pace of the reading is measured and she reads fluently and expressively, creating a sense of performance. Throughout the reading her eyes move from the text to the class and back again, seeking to ensure that pupils' attention is given to her reading of the poem.

When the reading is finished, she comments briefly on the way the poem is constructed before arranging a second reading by two pupils. She accepts that a second reading at this stage can be helpful no matter how straightforward the poem may appear to the teacher. The class is reading the text for the first time and pupils need more than one opportunity to come to terms with it, even though the teacher's own reading may have successfully communicated patterns of meaning and an overall coherence.

Teacher: Okay... you'll have some sort of idea of what the poem is about. I think it's maybe a bit easier for you to understand and follow what it's about if we divide it into two parts. Because what it does, it goes through a sort of question and answer routine, and it's obviously between two people and one person's asking all the questions and the other person is providing the answers. [The teacher has obviously decided to relay this information directly to the class in the form of an explanation, not to elicit it from them by means of questions and answers which would be more time-consuming.] ...so, em, two people who ...let's see ...any volunteers? [Lots of enthusiastic hands go up; it is important for her to choose two pupils who will read the poem well, otherwise interest and momentum may be lost.] ...All right... Julie and ...all right, Gregor. Julie and Gregor. Right now, let's have Gregor asking the questions and Julie providing the answers, so it's actually Julie who will start off. Okay? ...And you'll have to remember to speak up... Right... 'Welsh Incident'.

When Julie and Gregor have completed this second reading, the teacher does not launch directly into a discussion of the poem with the whole class. Instead she sets them a task to search for and organise information. Pupils return to a further close reading of the poem in order to find and note 'facts' about the incident. They are helped in this task by being told by the teacher that they are to think of themselves as policemen present at the scene and having to gather and report on the facts of the case. In a brief preparatory phase with the whole class the teacher elicits some of the facts from the narrative that pupils will be able to use in their own reports:

Teacher: Right. Now I think, now I think it's easier to follow the poem if you see... if you get this idea of questioning and answer because the whole thing is given a vague sort of title, 'Welsh Incident', and 'Incident' could mean anything that's happening, anything that has happened, and you're left wondering from the poem and from the questions and answers and by getting a little bit of information at a time, each time an answer is given to a question, em, you're allowed to build up some sort of picture. Now, what I want you to do just now is in your jotters to write down the facts you know about the incident, what facts you have actually established. Now if you were a police-man and you had been the one asking the questions and getting the information back in your little note-pad there, and you have to go and report to your sergeant at the police station, and he says, 'Right, what were the facts?', and these are the facts the actual facts that you were able to establish about the incident. What would you have jotted down in your little note-pad? Right? So I want you to read through the poem this time by yourselves and just jot down notes... fact one... Just till we get a start made, what facts have we got?... Heather?

Pupil [Heather]: There were all sorts of queer things.

Teacher: Right, all sorts of queer things. Now we've got a whole group of alien creatures, a group of alien creatures that have made an appearance – that's fact one. Can somebody give me fact two? [An open invitation; hands go up and the teacher points to an individual.]

Pupil: It happened at half-past three.

Teacher: Right. There's a good fact. [A reward to the pupil who answered.] A precise time. It happened at half-past three in the afternoon. What other facts do we have? [Another open invitation; the pace of the lesson gets brisker.]

Pupil: It was Easter.

Teacher: It was Easter Sunday. [In fact, it was Tuesday, but no one corrects her.]

Pupil: The colours were mostly nameless. [Difficult. How should she respond? Is this a fact?]

Teacher: Mostly nameless colours? Em, a bit vague, but it's still a fact. Any other facts?

Pupil: They hadn't a leg between them.

Teacher: Right, they hadn't a leg between them. They hadn't a leg to stand on, had they? Right, so it's facts like that. Try and see what... how many facts you can draw up on a list. See if you can reach twenty [a target to aim for], see if you can find twenty facts that you can tell us about the incident. Actual facts.... Right. You've got three whole minutes to do that just now. [A clear deadline; in fact they were given longer.]

The pupils settle down reasonably quickly and work quietly on the task. It is straightforward and has been clearly presented; they all know what they have to do. There is only a background murmur of noise as the class works. The teacher moves round between the desks checking on progress and quietly sorting out individual difficulties. Her manner has changed; she is quieter and more self-effacing. She then decides to intervene in order to check that everyone is making good progress and to give encouragement. To do this she moves back to the front of the classroom and directs pupils' attention from the task to herself. Her voice is again loud and her manner confident and authoritative:

Teacher: How many people have got as many as a dozen facts? [Several hands go up.] How many people have got more than a dozen? Anybody got as many as fifteen? [Again pupils respond.] Make it a long list. Imagine you were a policeman. What would you do? You're the one that's asking the questions... Write down the facts...

The class then returns to the task. It has been given a competitive edge – how many facts can they discover? When she is sure pupils are working quietly, the teacher writes on the blackboard in preparation for the next main phase of the lesson. She creates a simple framework to organise pupils' replies when they respond to the questions she will ask, after the present task has been completed. She writes the heading 'Facts' and then two further sub-headings – 'Incident' and (on the lower half of the board) 'Creatures'. She then moves back unobtrusively to the pupils' desks to watch them writing and offer occasional comments. When she judges the time is right, she brings the task to an end and makes the transition to the next phase of the lesson – an extended question and answer phase that will use the pupils' written notes as a starting point. For this transition she again returns to the focal point at the front of the class near the blackboard:

Teacher: Right, can you just finish at that point? Because probably, all together, we'll have all the facts, different people will have different facts. One group had eighteen, anybody get more than eighteen? [Hands go up.] Twenty?... twenty-one? Good!.... All right, what I want to do is to organise the facts a bit. Rather than just saying, 'Well, let's look at all the facts that are in the poem', let's organise them into two lots of facts. Facts about the *incident* [pointing to the blackboard], facts about what actually happened here in this particular place, and facts about the *creatures*, because the whole incident is concerned with these strange creatures that have come up on this place. So let's divide the facts into two lots. Who can give me some facts about the incident? Facts about *what* happened, *where* it happened, *when* it happened [she writes these key words on the blackboard]. I mean if they... where, when, what, who [writing]... I don't know if you are given the information about when and what... well, *what* you are, yes... where, when, what, who [reading what she has written]. Can somebody fill in the facts that we've got about those things? [Hands go up.] Right, Karen?

Pupil [Karen]: It happened at half-past three on Easter Tuesday.

Teacher: Right, three-thirty, Easter Tuesday was it? [Realising her earlier mistake?] Right... [writing on the blackboard]. Right, anything else? Anything about where?

Pupil: Near the sea.

Teacher: Right, it was on the beach.

Pupil: The sun was shining. [This is not really an appropriate answer.]

Teacher: Em, all right, we'll add that... 'Sun shining', that tells us what sort of day it was. [She reads from the blackboard] 'Three-thirty Easter Tuesday, sun shining, happened on the beach.' *What* happened?

Pupil: Creatures came out the sea.

Teacher: Right, 'Creatures came out of the sea' [she speaks slowly as she writes]. 'Actually on the beach.' We could have added something else about *where*.... Where?.... On what beach, in other words?

Pupil: On a Welsh beach. [This is probably not the reply she was expecting.]

Teacher: Right, a Welsh beach. Can you be even more specific?

Pupil: Criccieth.

Teacher: Criccieth. Anybody saying 'A Welsh beach', they could give even more detail by saying Criccieth... I don't know if that's how it's spelled [writing]. We'll put it up like that just now. Right, what other facts do we know about the incident? *Who* was present?

Pupil: The mayor.

Pupil: The mayor and the band.

Teacher: Right, the mayor, the band, and...?

Pupil: The townfolk.

Teacher: The townspeople and...?

Pupil: The creatures.

Teacher: Right, it wasn't just the townspeople of this particular town...?

Pupil: For miles around.

Teacher: Right, it's the populations of [reading] 'Pwllheli, Criccieth, Portmadoc, Borth, Tremadoc, Penrhyndeudraeth.' In other words townspeople from other villages.... Right, could we add other information about what happened? It wasn't just that the creatures came out of the sea or came out of the sea caves, what else happened?

Pupil: They went back into the sea.

Pupil: The band played.

Teacher: Right, the band played.

Pupil: The mayor twisted his fingers on his chain.

Teacher: Right, what did the mayor.... Right [The teacher's use of the word 'right' is partly a mannerism, but it is also a management device to catch eyes and bring wandering attention back to the task in hand]... he thinks it's a really big incident. Here are these strange creatures and they happen to choose his village to appear in, so he's all decked out... is there anything that suggests that, em, that this isn't just accidental, that you know that they've deliberately gone out of their way to make preparations for these creatures, that they were expecting these creatures, that something has been arranged? Are there any details?

Pupil: The mayor addressed them.

Teacher: Right, the mayor addressed them, and as well as addressing them, how's he prepared for it?

Pupil: He's got all his special clothes.

Teacher: He's got all his finery on. His chain of office on and addresses them. How does he address them? Just for good measure?

Pupil: He welcomes them.

Teacher: Right, what language does he use?

Pupil: Welsh and English.

Teacher: Two languages. He uses Welsh and English. Maybe he's playing safe and he thinks, 'Ah, well, they don't understand English, maybe they'll understand Welsh,' so he tries them in two languages. But anyway, the band is playing, so they've got, they've got the band there for this special occasion. They've got all the villagers from the villages round about for this special occasion and it's almost as if they are waiting for the sea creatures to come towards them. So [writing on the blackboard] the band played, the mayor spoke to them... and what did the creatures do?

Pupil: They rolled on to the sand.

Teacher: Right, they came on to the sand, and then what? Disappeared in a puff of blue smoke? What?

Pupil: They disappeared back into the sea.

Teacher: Right, it suggests that they just wandered off into the sea and disappeared, because they made their way *slowly*, it says, em, '...moving seaward silently at a snail's pace', so they just move off, move to the sea. Except one other thing happens that seems to cause a bit of excitement. What is that one other thing? The real incident that people obviously got quite worked up about? [Hands go up.] John?

Pupil [John]: It made a noise.

Teacher: Right, it made a noise. One of the creatures made a noise, and that seems to be the big thing. It says, em, [reading] 'But at last the most odd, indescribable thing of all, which hardly one man there could see for wonder did something recognisably a something. Well, what? It made a noise.' ... right, so the highlight of the incident is the creature makes a noise, one of the creatures makes a noise. Right, there are some of the facts about the incident then: [reading from the blackboard] it takes place on the beach, it's on a Welsh beach, it's actually on the beach at Criccieth, it happens at three-thirty in the afternoon on Easter Tuesday and it's a beautiful day, the sun's shining. The creatures come out of the sea-caves but they're expected, they're waited for. The mayor is there from the village, the band of the village is there, the townspeople and other villagers are there. The band is playing to them to welcome them, the mayor speaks to them in two languages. Then we go on to the scene, but in all this amazement from people, one of the creatures makes a noise, and that gets everybody quite excited. Right, what we've found out...

if that's what we've found out about the *incident*, what have we found out about the *creatures*?

The teacher has successfully used the framework on the blackboard together with the organising questions – what? where? when? who? – to build up a description of the scene. As different pupils have responded to her questions, she has written key words and phrases from their replies on the blackboard to act as a reminder and has teased out some of the important details of the description. And, in order to reinforce what is being said, she occasionally points to words written there. The attention of the class has been held throughout and most pupils have participated enthusiastically.

This phase of the lesson continues and the teacher's questions direct pupils' attention next to the creatures themselves. It quickly emerges that there is abundant information from the storyteller about what the creatures were not like, but little that is positive or precise. The teacher summarises the position at the end of the phase as follows:

Teacher: Right, let's take a look at these things. Look at them on the board there just now. Here is the information we have about the creatures. Let's go over it. They've got no legs, they're strange, they're weird, some are colourful, some are colour-less. They *weren't* mermaids or dragons, they made a noise, but it was an indescribable sort of noise. They were all different sizes, they were solid, they were all shapes, no two were alike and they moved slowly. Now, from that, how good a picture would you say you have been given of the creatures? Who could just now quite confidently put up their hand and say, 'I could draw one of those'?... [Not clear. There are a number of responses.] ...It's left, in other words... what Karen is saying is quite true... it's left to your imagination really. You're not given enough detail to get an exact picture of the creatures, because it's left to your imagination what colour you make them, what size you make them, what shape you make them, because any shape, any size, any colour fits, so it's a very, very vague description. Em, how do you know... well, first of all, when people saw these creatures, when all the people that saw, that were gathered together, when they saw those creatures, were they terrified?
Pupil: No. They greeted them.
Teacher: Right, what evidence... what evidence have you got for saying they weren't terrified? What would they have done, if they had been terrified?
Pupil: Run away.
Teacher: Right, they would have run away.
Pupil: They were interested in what was going on.

Teacher: Right, they were fascinated... they were intrigued. [The teacher extends the pupil's answer with more emphatic vocabulary.] So they weren't terrified. The creatures, they didn't make them want to run away. They wanted to watch them and they were wondering at them, at the amazing different colours, sizes and shapes and so on. How do you know, though ...there's one piece of evidence that suggests one person anyway was nervous.

Pupil: The mayor.

Teacher: Right, the mayor was nervous. How do we know the mayor was nervous?

Pupil: He was fiddling with his chain.

Teacher: Right, he's waiting to speak to the creatures. He's got the chain of office round his neck [gesture] and he's standing fiddling with his chain of office because he's obviously nervous. But it's apparently because he feels this chain's very important...

[After the exploration of how the onlookers and especially the mayor felt, the teacher moves on to consider briefly the characters of the storyteller and the listener in the poem and soon afterwards the lesson ends.]

This is a purposeful lesson with a clear sense of direction. The teacher's behaviour is confident and authoritative and she moves the lesson forward at a brisk, but not a confusing pace. Momentum is never lost. The class works hard and responds positively and well. From the pupils' point of view the lesson does not lack variety. They listen to the readings of the poem and follow in the text; they re-read it carefully themselves and make notes about its content; they listen to the teacher's questions, think and respond, accepting the teacher's rules for answering only when their turn is indicated; they look at and read what is written on the blackboard; they listen to other pupils' responses to the questions.

The teacher's classroom behaviour is varied too. She uses her face and gesture expressively and during the note-taking phase she moves about the room to ensure that everyone is making progress. Her voice is clearly audible and is varied in range. She emphasises and repeats key words and phrases. Although her questions concentrate attention on the 'facts' of the poem, she manages to communicate a sense of her own enjoyment and encourages pupils' responses to her questions. She makes simple but effective use of the blackboard to organise and highlight points made by pupils when they answer her questions.

In the course of the lesson the class has been kept busy and interested, and the teacher herself has worked hard (although she did conserve some nervous energy during the note-taking phase). The class were given a clear task to complete and a large number of children participated in the lesson, especially by answering questions. However, as the transcript shows, pupils' oral contributions (in contrast to the teacher's) are never extended. The lesson is not only directed, but is dominated by the teacher. As a result pupils have been offered a model of how an experienced reader can probe for meaning and reflect on a text, and how responses can be organised into a coherent logical form.

To conclude, then, if you wish to examine critically your own classroom performance in the use of the directive mode, you will find a checklist of questions derived from the preceding discussion in figure 2.1. Unless it is possible to audio-record (or even better video-record) a lesson, it is obviously difficult to evaluate your own teaching performance. Some of the questions on the checklist, therefore, may be better answered with the help of a colleague who has observed the lesson (perhaps a more experienced teacher). However, it is still possible for you to apply the checklist to your own day-to-day teaching, as best you can. The checklist is intended to be used flexibly; you do not have to work your way through it systematically, item by item. (The appraisal of teaching is discussed in detail in chapter eight.)

Checklist of skills – the directive mode

THE DIRECTIVE MODE OF TEACHING

Planning the lesson
How successful was I in choosing interesting subject-matter and materials for this particular group of pupils?
Was the lesson pitched at an appropriate level of difficulty?
Was there sufficient variety in the lesson to maintain pupils' interest?

Implementing the lesson
How much did I talk?
Was there sufficient variety in my own voice and behaviour?
Were my explanations clear enough?
How varied and effective was my questioning?
How successful was I in responding to pupils and making use of their contributions to the lesson?

Managing the classroom
Did I present myself to the class with sufficient confidence and authority?
Have I established clear rules for working in this mode?
Did I 'reward' and 'punish' some pupils more than others?
Was the pace of the lesson appropriate?
Was there a clear sense of purpose and direction to the lesson?

Evaluating progress
Were the pupils interested in the lesson? Did they co-operate and participate?
What was taught? What was learned?
How successful was I in monitoring the progress of the lesson and in picking up cues from pupils' behaviour?
What unplanned decisions did I take which changed the course of the lesson?

Figure 2.1

Chapter three

Discussing

It is not uncommon for teachers to describe the kind of lesson examined in the previous case study as a discussion. In a subsequent lesson the teacher in charge might well have said to the same class, 'In yesterday's lesson, you remember, we discussed the poem "Welsh Incident", now today ...' In contrast, the transcript itself clearly demonstrates that there is very little happening in the lesson (worthwhile though the activities may be) that can be described as genuine discussion. Talking is dominated by the teacher. Pupils are given opportunities to answer questions and to respond, but, as we observed, they make few, if any, extended contributions to the lesson themselves.

The main purpose of the discursive mode of teaching, on the other hand, is to increase pupils' self-confidence, fluency and skills in oral discussion. In this context it should be the pupils, not the teacher, who do most of the talking. As teacher, you have to control your own eagerness to contribute to and perhaps dominate a discussion and ensure instead that you create a context and a climate that encourage pupils to participate. What, then, are the mode's distinctive features?

The characteristics of the discursive mode

Discursive teaching does not presuppose any particular form of classroom organisation. It is possible, for example, to arrange your classroom in much the same way as for the lesson exploring 'Welsh Incident'. The normal procedure in such a context is for the teacher to choose a contentious issue for discussion (the amount of freedom that teenagers should be allowed, for instance) and to throw the topic open for whole class discussion. Your role as teacher may be initially as catalyst to get discussion going, perhaps too as neutral chairperson (especially if the debate is fluent and lively), and perhaps, if debate flags, as devil's advocate. You may have to try deliberately to bring quieter pupils into the discussion and sometimes you will have to repeat what one pupil has said so that the whole class can hear clearly what the contribution was. In the main you will find your role is that of manager, facilitator and occasional contributor.

From the pupil's point of view, though, the classroom rules in this context are not unlike those for directive teaching. If you want to say something, you will probably have to put up your hand and wait your turn. You are also likely to spend most of the lesson listening to others (though not necessarily the teacher) rather than speaking yourself. For the self-confident, extrovert child the mode offers, when interpreted in this form, an opportunity to seize the limelight and dominate the debate. For the less confident child, on the other hand, there is the struggle to speak up and be heard and the embarrassment of becoming the focus of the whole class's attention. And obviously in a single lesson it is unlikely that all members of the class will be able to make a major contribution to the discussion.

Many experienced teachers will quickly lose patience with the kind of lesson that has been described. In some classes, just as in traditional directive lessons, pupils are not prepared to accept the rules and conventions of this kind of formal discursive lesson. Opinions are shouted across the room with great gusto, sometimes in a simultaneous chorus. Few pupils seem prepared to listen to points of view that conflict with their own values and beliefs. Some are happy to escape altogether and retreat into a personal dream world untouched by the lesson's debate. At its worst such a lesson is a travesty of a discussion; it becomes an incoherent babel of opinions. Even at its best, when discussion is well organised and tolerant, with a large number of pupils participating, a sense of dissatisfaction remains.

Do lessons like these help pupils to develop an essential life-skill? Perhaps as adults they will have to attend different kinds of public meeting; they will have to sit and listen intelligently; they will have to take their turn to ask questions or make a point ; they will need to have the courage and self-confidence to stand up and say their piece. But such occasions for most will be rare. By participating in a whole-class discussion, it is true pupils are given the opportunity to listen to and perhaps to interact with their peers, to realise that their own beliefs and life experiences either match those of others or contrast and conflict with them. And this may be an important part of growing up, especially in adolescence, when your point of view may be shifting and you feel strongly about important issues. But, that said, to work in smaller groups with, say, up to six members, is more manageable for the teacher, at least as far as controlling the discussion is concerned, and less inhibiting for many children. And it is more likely to be a helpful preparation for life beyond school.

If, then, you choose to work with pupils organised in groups rather than with the whole class as a single unit, what would be the characteristic features of the discursive mode? How much does it have in common with directive teaching and in what ways can it be contrasted with it? To answer these questions we can begin by considering a hypothetical lesson in the discursive mode which would involve pupils exploring a poem similar to 'Welsh Incident' which featured in the previous case study of directive teaching.

First, it is important to emphasise that a discursive lesson is unlikely to consist of a single phase alone. In other words, it would be an unusual class that simply entered the room, sat down in groups and, perhaps as a result of some kind of written instructions and materials, immediately embarked on a discussion. It would be surprising, too, if, finally, when the lesson bell rang, they packed up their belongings and departed without any guidance from the teacher. Almost certainly there will be some kind of directive introduction when the task is explained and organised, and also some kind of conclusion before pupils leave. The teacher's skills in planning and making use of these initial and concluding phases will be discussed fully in the next section.

However, when the pupils are actually engaged in the main phase of the lesson, discussing different aspects of the poem, as teacher, you will have much less control than in directive teaching over the pace and direction of the lesson. You may well give pupils deadlines and objectives to work towards – 'You will have about twenty minutes to do this, so make sure you agree on the answers to the three main questions in that time...' – but clearly you will not be able to take the lesson forward yourself in a way that would have been possible in directive teaching. Your role as teacher is no longer that of performer. You have to be much more self-effacing. You are likely to move round the groups, ensuring that all are making satisfactory progress, listening in to what pupils have to say, perhaps asking an occasional question or making a contribution to the discussion. In the process you will probably burn up much less nervous energy than in directive teaching, but you will still have to remain alert, ensuring that all pupils remain purposefully involved in the lesson and 'on task'.

For pupils, on the other hand, there is a much more active role to play, when working in this mode. It is true, as a pupil, you have not been involved in the process of choosing the poem which is to be discussed, the teacher may well have distributed written questions to guide the discussion, and deadlines have been set for you to meet, but none the less there is considerably more freedom open to you to explore the poem in your own way than was the case before. Now you can ask the questions you want to ask and you can ask them in your own way. Provided that you understand and are prepared to accept the rules and conventions that underpin group discussion, you have considerably more opportunity to develop the lesson at your own pace and in the direction in which you want it to go. Some pupils may well still be quiet listeners and some will participate in the discussion less than others, but they will all be able to ask questions and begin to contribute as their confidence and interest grow.

It is likely that one member of the group will have been appointed or elected as chairperson and another will have been given the responsibility of acting as secretary to take notes and record the main points made by the other members of the group. If time allows it, the teacher may include a reporting back session at the conclusion of the lesson when the secretaries in turn give their summaries of each group's main conclusions. This in turn could provoke further discussion in the more formal context of the whole class.

It is possible that desks will be laid out in the classroom in the traditional manner, singly or in pairs, facing the blackboard. In this case there will be a certain amount of initial noise and confusion as pupils move desks and chairs to form the groups in which they will be working. If, on the other hand, the teacher makes considerable use of group work, it is likely that the room will be set out in such a way as to ensure that work can begin with the minimum of noise and fuss. Groups of four can be formed quickly by pairs of children moving their chairs in a half-circle to work with the pair sitting immediately behind them. Or the room may be set out more flexibly with desks arranged in groups so that children are already facing each other across the tables rather than facing the teacher at the front of the room.

Despite the orderly and purposeful picture that has been presented, and the growing acceptance of the importance of discussion in the English curriculum, the discursive mode of teaching has not yet established itself in schools and classrooms with the same degree of popularity and general acceptance as traditional directive teaching. The teacher's apparent loss of control over the development of the lesson and the self-effacing role that is essential to its success seem to provoke uncertainty and anxiety in many teachers. And sometimes they feel less than confident that worthwhile outcomes have been achieved in discursive lessons. After all, children seem ready enough to chatter to each other on their way to school, in the playground, and between lessons. Why endeavour to extend the process to the classroom itself? There appears to be no problem in getting children to talk; the problem, as many teachers perceive it, lies in trying to keep a class quiet.

Clearly many children do show themselves to be orally fluent and self-confident in school (and beyond) with certain kinds of subject-matter, in certain contexts and with particular kinds of audience. In some circumstances they may well possess sophisticated and varied skills and strategies in order to report, describe, persuade, control, or simply listen. And it is not necessarily the child who scores high marks in reading and writing tasks that earns praise and respect for spoken activities in the classroom. Often, in fact, quite the opposite is true. If this is so, opportunities to excel in discussion may provide important sources of motivation and self-esteem for many pupils who are less successful in other areas of the curriculum, especially those involving reading and writing.

In the long term, however, it does not seem to be sensible for pupils to go on practising in the classroom only those activities and skills in which they have already demonstrated a high level of confidence and success. What most children need in this field – as I argued in the opening chapter – is explicit help in talking about subjects which are *not* part of their everyday lives and understanding, in unusual and probably more formal contexts, and with people who are unknown to them and may not necessarily share their own assumptions and beliefs. They need help with communicating for a range of purposes and in listening intelligently and sensitively as a discussion develops. We should recognise, as research in fact suggests, that young people appear to be more at ease with 'listener-related' talk, where the emphasis is on relating to other people (especially those of their own age group who they know well), than on situations that are 'information-related', where they have to concentrate on communicating clearly and explicitly a 'message' of some kind, especially when the setting is unfamiliar and perhaps formal. It appears, too, that pupils are more likely to be fluent and confident in 'short-turn' dialogue, where a variety of individuals contribute quickly and briefly to a conversation, than with 'extended' involvement when you have to develop or 'unpack' an argument, explanation, or description (see, for example, Brown, Anderson, Shillcock, and Yule 1984: 11 and 15).

The skills of discursive teaching

What personal qualities and skills, then, do you need to possess or acquire as a teacher to ensure that your pupils develop their confidence and expertise in contributing to and learning from small-group discussion? As in the previous consideration of traditional directive teaching, it is important to take account of a number of interrelated factors – the role and personal qualities of the teacher, the rules and conventions that have to be learned and accepted by pupils, and the ways in which lessons can be planned and presented. Certainly success in this mode of teaching has to be worked for; it will not come about fortuitously. As we have already indicated, pupils will not normally spontaneously organise themselves into groups and begin to discuss. In fact, sometimes you find the early stages of group discussion can be a disheartening experience; pupils appear reluctant to talk and seem to view the whole enterprise with suspicion. As in any new venture, they need to be given time and help in order to acquire the appropriate inter-personal and linguistic skills, and to understand and accept the classroom rules that apply to the mode. And teachers in their turn have to develop skills in presenting, organising and stimulating discussion, if the mode is to succeed.

From the teacher's point of view, classroom discussion, as with any mode of teaching, has to be prepared and planned for. For example, you will have to take account of the following factors which are likely to influence your lesson:

(i)   You will have to try to ensure that the topic or theme which is chosen is interesting and worthwhile, and arises naturally from some aspect of the continuing work of the class.

(ii) Almost certainly, before pupils begin the actual business of discussion, you will need to plan a directive introduction to the lesson, when the nature and purposes of the discussion are explained and routines are organised. You may also decide at this stage to 'prime' the pupils in some way, stimulating interest by presenting, for example, a variety of conflicting viewpoints, emphasising a particular point of view, or getting pupils to contribute their own preliminary ideas as a preparation for the discussion to come. And it may be important, too, at this initial stage, to give pupils clear targets to aim for and deadlines to meet.

(iii) You may have to pre-plan the composition of the groups, deciding who will (or will not) work with whom, and appointing or electing a suitable chairperson and secretary for each group. Depending on the purposes of the lesson, you will sometimes want pupils to work in 'friendship groups', whereas on other occasions it may be important to bring individuals together to form random or mixed-ability groups, or to ensure that boys and girls work together.

(iv) Finally, you may have to rearrange classroom furniture, if the layout of the room is inappropriate to this mode of teaching and learning.

Your main aim in any introductory phase to a lesson will be to provide a structure or framework so that the class can become involved in the actual business of talking and listening as speedily as possible. This structure is partly conceptual – providing a framework of ideas – and partly managerial – creating an organised context in which the class can work. But once you have achieved your aim and the directive phase of the lesson comes to an end, the main responsibility for talking will shift away from you on to the pupils themselves. And, inevitably, in the process, your role as a teacher will change in important ways.

If the pupils understand and accept the rules of discursive teaching, there will no need for you to continue to dominate or direct. This does not mean you should retire to your desk to mark books or act as a spectator. Pupils need to be aware that you are still involved in the lesson, perhaps participating in some respect, and monitoring the progress of the different groups. So perceptual awareness, as in any mode of teaching, is again an important quality for you to possess. As well as going round the different groups, listening in to a discussion and contributing to it, you will have to be able to abruptly switch your attention, picking up evidence of restlessness or flagging interest from across the room, intervening with a loud authoritative voice to get an individual or a group back to work, or reminding the class about the deadlines you have set.

It is better if you move round the classroom slowly and purposefully so that you can give adequate attention to each group (some inexperienced teachers have been known to orbit the classroom once every two minutes). And it is important, too, when you are listening to a group, and perhaps contributing to the discussion, that you position yourself in such a way that you are able to keep the rest of the class within your field of vision. In this way you can pick up and comment on behaviour problems as they arise. At the same time, when you are working with a particular group, you will need to convey to its members (though not explicitly) that your role is no longer that of traditional, didactic teacher.

It is best, for example, if you do not tower above the group, but come down to their level by sitting with them or squatting beside a desk. When you speak, your voice should be quieter and your manner more informal. Your behaviour should show that you are interested in hearing what different pupils have to say. When you ask a question, it is genuinely because something in the discussion is not clear, or because you want further information; you are not testing or assessing. You contribute to the discussion yourself because you believe you have something important or of interest to add, or because the group seems to have overlooked an argument or an alternative point of view. In one sense, you are not involved in the discussion as 'the teacher', but simply as an extra member of the group, contributing with the rest on an equal footing. At the same time, though, in a different sense, you still have to remain aware of your continuing professional role with the group. You do still in fact remain 'the teacher', because you are showing pupils, by the way you behave and respond, how an experienced and skilled speaker listens and contributes to a discussion. You are not presenting yourself to the group as an authority on the subject being discussed, someone, that is, whose opinions have to be noted and respected. But you are, none the less, acting as a model to help pupils to understand better how the processes of discussion operate successfully.

Inevitably, if thirty children are arranged in groups and are participating in a lively exchange of views, a high level of noise is likely to be created. Beginning teachers in particular will find such noise threatening. There is the worry that other teachers working nearby will be disturbed, or that the lesson will be interrupted by a more experienced colleague who believes that your pupils are getting out of hand. As regards the level of noise, different teachers obviously have different toleration thresholds. Some experienced teachers are content to be surrounded by quite a high level of noise, whereas others insist on a much quieter classroom, no matter what mode of teaching is being adopted. It is only reasonable that your classes should know what will count as an acceptable level of noise in your classroom, and you need to make this threshold part of your system of rules for this mode. Pupils need to be warned about the problem at the outset of a lesson, when you are establishing or reinforcing your rules, and you can give additional reminders and warnings as the lesson develops. The actual level of noise which is acceptable can be established pragmatically. You intervene clearly and firmly as a directive teacher when the noise level seems to be approaching or goes beyond your own notional threshold.

If you allow the lesson to be stopped by the ringing of the interval bell, obviously the discussion will not have been brought to an acceptable conclusion. In addition, you will almost certainly have created management problems for yourself. You will probably still have to collect in any materials that have been used in the lesson, perhaps rearrange desks for the next incoming class, and give out any final instructions to the departing pupils. You should obviously do your best to ensure that all these routines are carried out before pupils make their dash for the next lesson or the playground.

As we indicated earlier, if time allows it, the secretaries of the different groups can also report back to the class in a final plenary session. They can give summaries of the conclusions reached by the group and answer any questions from other members of the class. A formal conclusion like this brings together the two interpretations of the discursive mode that were presented at the outset – discussion as a whole class and discussion in small groups. It gives pupils the opportunity to experience a more formal mode of presentation with the teacher acting as organiser and neutral chairperson.

Until now we have presented the teacher's perspective on the discursive mode. Obviously it is equally important to explore also the pupil's point of view and to consider the skills and understandings every child must acquire if this mode of teaching and learning is to succeed.

Generally speaking, as we argued earlier, when pupils work in groups, positive motivation is easier to achieve in this mode than is often the case in directive teaching. Pupils often indicate that they believe that discussion is not 'real work' and that they enjoy the activities it involves. And in the arrangements that have been described they feel that they have a more important part to play in influencing the direction and pace of classroom events. The teacher will have created a context and a purpose for the discussion, will have set goals and deadlines, and will have established the procedures and ground rules already described. These rules and procedures may be essential to a lesson's success, but, from the pupil's perspective, they are imposed from outside. There are, in addition, other rules and conventions, intrinsic to the nature of successful discussion, which have to be learned and accepted, if pupils are going to relate successfully to and interact with the other members of their group.

As a pupil, there are obvious criteria you know you have to meet. You realise, for example, that you are expected to contribute to the discussion, not merely act as a passive listener. You probably recognise too (perhaps because the teacher has emphasised it) that the chairperson is given some authority and has the responsibility for controlling and directing the discussion. On the other hand, your prior experience of 'discussions' at home or with friends may lead you to try to impose your beliefs and conclusions on the rest of the group with some energy, rather than being prepared to listen to others, to reflect, and argue your case. None the less the teacher has probably emphasised that not everyone can speak at the same time; you have to wait your turn and allow others to have their say (a situation not unlike the one you have experienced in a directive classroom).

More subtly, though, you have to learn in addition how to concentrate on the development of the discussion and how to make a relevant and appropriate contribution to it. You have to watch, as well as listen, and pick up important non-verbal cues from the rest of the group. Participating in the developing debate is not merely a matter of overcoming any natural embarrassment, or reluctance to contribute, and being prepared to tough out any hostility or ridicule from your peers. There is also the problem of knowing how to say what you want to say, and recognising what strategies you can use to get a fair hearing. How, for example, do you express yourself when you are trying to make a major point? How do you find an acceptable way of disagreeing with someone else? How do you try to obtain further information from another speaker? How do you set about supporting another person's argument? Should you try to bring the more reluctant members of the group into the discussion yourself or is that the responsibility of the chairperson?

As a pupil, you have at some point to try to find acceptable answers to all these questions if you are to feel that you are making progress and developing your expertise. The teacher, too, is faced by the corresponding dilemma of deciding whether to allow pupils to find their own answers 'naturally', on the job, as their experience of the discursive mode grows, or whether some form of intervention by the teacher to explain and demonstrate is necessary or helpful at some point in pupils' learning careers.

Planning and presenting discursive lessons

Classroom discussion can obviously be directed towards any aspect of the English curriculum and can be used with classes of any age and level of achievement. Discussion can involve responses to a text (or part of a text), a subject that is to form the main element in an eventual writing task, or an issue that has arisen from the exploration of a topic or theme. The examples that follow are taken from the classroom work of both experienced and inexperienced teachers. They are intended to show how the characteristic features of the discursive mode, considered in the earlier sections, come to life in the reality of a classroom, and to illustrate the professional skills that are essential to its successful use.

The nature of the task

An earlier case study described how an experienced teacher explored the poem 'Welsh Incident' in a traditional directive lesson. As I showed at the beginning of this chapter, it is possible to organise both your mode of approach and the use of a literary text in such a way that a class is given much more freedom and responsibility in a lesson. Pupils can be much more active in exploring the meanings of a selected text, their own responses to it, and the ways in which the author has achieved particular effects. But, as earlier discussion has emphasised, this involvement can only be achieved if pupils already understand and accept the rules and conventions of the discursive mode and have learned how to approach a literary text by means of group discussion.

For example, the poem 'The Companion' was used in this way with a mixed class of 13-year-olds (Yevtushenko 1962). The poem describes initially an air attack carried out by the invading German army on a civilian train in Russia during the Second World War. It then goes on to describe at greater length the relationship that develops between a small boy and girl, who were travelling on the train but until then were unknown to each other. As they set out to walk the rest of the journey after the destruction of the train, the boy (who is the narrator) assumes that the girl will be a hindrance to him and hold him back. In fact, the opposite turns out to be the case; she proves to be the tougher and more resilient of the two and he is the one whose strength and determination begin to falter.

At the beginning of the lesson pupils were given copies of the poem and the teacher read it aloud to them. They then had an opportunity to read it again themselves silently. There then followed a short teacher-led question and answer phase in which the teacher established the date of the narrative (1941), its location (Russia), and its context (the Nazi invasion). This was achieved by teasing the information out of the pupils, using their hazy existing knowledge, and directing their attention to names and references in the poem – the name of the author himself, for example, and the girl in the narrative (Katya). Once the context of the story had been established, though, the teacher organised the class into groups so that pupils could discuss some of the key issues in the poem themselves. With older and more experienced classes it is often possible for groups to set their own agenda, but on this occasion, with a younger class that had not much recent experience of group work, the teacher provided a framework for the discussion with the following key questions:

(i)   What is the story of the poem? What happened after the train had been bombed? (A basic initial question. Each group has to talk its way to an understanding of what happens in the unfolding of the narrative of the poem.)

(ii) What sort of boy was the story-teller? (Pupils have to look closely at what they are told explicitly and to read 'between the lines', inferring aspects of his character from what he says and does.)

(iii) What sort of girl was Katya? (They have to chart the changes in the story-teller's perceptions of her as the narrative develops.)

(iv) What does the story-teller learn as a result of the events he describes? In your opinion, is what he learns true? (The most contentious question and the one that stimulated most discussion. Apart from having to sum up the 'message' of the poem about preconceived sexual stereotypes, pupils are asked to evaluate this message and judge it in the light of their own experiences and assumptions.)

The provision of these questions helps to give pupils a clearer sense of purpose and direction; it provides a framework for their discussions. The questions are obviously general and open; they are not presented in the form of detailed reading comprehension or interpretation questions which pupils have to work through methodically. Nor do groups have to provide answers that the teacher will agree with or approve of.

The lesson lasted some 70 minutes in all and concluded with a final plenary phase where one individual from each group reported back with their answers to one question only. These individual reports stimulated further whole-class discussion chaired by the teacher. About 25–30 minutes were needed to complete the group discussions; about 15–20 minutes were spent on the introductory and concluding phases.

The second example relates to a lesson taught by a less experienced teacher as part of a unit of work exploring the reading and writing of short stories with a supernatural theme. The class involved was a high-achieving group of 15-year-olds (boys and girls). Before the lesson in question took place, the class had already read a selection of stories by established writers and examined their style and technique with the teacher (for example, 'The Monkey's Paw' by W. W. Jacobs, 'A Night at a Cottage' by Richard Hughes and stories by Ray Bradbury). They had then been given the task of writing their own stories with a supernatural theme on a topic of their own choice. To give them further guidance the teacher had provided a checklist which identified the qualities that had emerged in earlier lessons as being important in the writing of an effective short story – the limited length and the necessary compression this involves, a successful but not complicated central idea for the plot, a limited number of characters and a limited amount of description, and a possible surprise or twist in the ending. (See appendix B.)

The main purpose of the group discussion in the lesson to be described was to read and respond to the stories the pupils themselves had written and to offer critical comments and encouragement to their authors. The lesson again began with a short directive phase to remind the class about the purposes of the story they had written and to explain the task they were to be given. In groups they were to begin by silently reading each other's stories. Then, using the checklist of qualities already provided and their own responses, they were to discuss each story in turn, considering what they liked about it, its strengths and weaknesses. As a group they were then to decide which one of the stories they considered to be the most successful. This selected story would be taken forward to the final plenary phase of the lesson with the whole class which would involve a second public reading and a discussion of the story's special merits.

A certain amount of reorganisation and movement was necessary to form groups of four or five (customary groupings, not created for this purpose), but this was done quickly and efficiently. The teacher was confident – both he and the pupils knew what was to be done and his instructions were clear. Some confusion was caused because a small number of pupils had left their stories at home and this meant some further rearrangement of the groups was necessary. Once this had been sorted out, the class settled down to a phase of quiet, concentrated reading with occasional whispered comments and questions from pupil to pupil. The teacher simply sat and watched during the first part of this phase, and then, when stories became free, he too began reading at random.

Once he sensed that this phase was coming to an end (some pupils had obviously finished reading and there was increased restlessness and talking), he told the class to begin their discussions of the stories as soon as they were ready. Once this next phase got under way, discussion was lively and good humoured. The teacher moved round from group to group, listening in and making occasional comments. Pupils obviously knew what was required of them in this mode of work and the teacher had to intervene only occasionally to remind them about the level of noise. The class responded to these warnings immediately. A deadline of twenty minutes had been set by the teacher for this phase, but in fact it went on for longer.

After warning the class that they would need to bring their discussions to an end and make their final selections, the teacher made a purposeful, confident transition to the final phase of the lesson. He took up a central position, sitting on the teacher's desk at the front, and ensured that he had the attention of the whole class. He then went on to ask each group in turn to nominate their selected stories and arranged for the authors to read them aloud to the class. The first story described how the writer had picked up a strange, silent hitchhiker on a lonely, desolate stretch of road, and how the experience had been repeated with exactly the same figure a year later. The second story was initially more prosaic with the writer sitting alone at home struggling unsuccessfully to write a ghost story as an English composition, when uncanny events started to take place. The standard of writing (and performance in reading the stories aloud) was high. After each reading, the teacher commented on the qualities of the story himself and asked for questions and responses from other members of the class. These came from a variety of individuals, and as a result the lesson ran out of time. It was not possible to hear a story from each of the groups before the lesson ended.

The lesson concluded, therefore, with the promise that the readings would be continued next day. Once all the selected stories had been heard and discussed, pupils would be able to work on the final versions of their own stories and take account of the comments that had been made. Finally, pupils moved back to their original seats with some noise and chatter and the lesson ended. It lasted one hour. The introduction took about 10 minutes, with the main phase of silent reading and discussion taking about 30 minutes, and the final readings with plenary discussion taking about 15 minutes.

Priming

As I argued earlier, it seems unreasonable to expect any class to sit down and begin a discussion without any help or support being offered by the teacher. In the previous two examples this support took the form of the teacher establishing a context and sense of purpose at the beginning of the lesson, and by providing appropriate guidelines for each discussion. The term 'priming' can be applied to any form of initial help offered by the teacher to enable a class to begin a discussion with a better understanding of the topic or a clearer idea both of what is expected of them and of what is to be achieved. But, most especially, it involves the giving of information which helps pupils to approach their task in a more informed and purposeful way.

For example, as part of a unit of work exploring the theme 'Freedom and Responsibility', a senior secondary school class was asked to consider the rights and wrongs of compelling people by law to wear safety belts when travelling by car. The main topic for pupils to discuss was the likely change in the law in the United Kingdom affecting children travelling in rear seats (1989). Should parents have the right to decide for themselves whether their children should travel in a safety seat or harness when travelling by car or should this decision be imposed on them? Are there important differences between short journeys (like the journey to school) and travelling longer distances? Is the safety of a child more important than considerations of individual freedom?

As with any emotive topic, there is a danger that a discussion will provide pupils with an opportunity simply to air the prejudices they have absorbed from home and neighbourhood without much reflection. The purpose of priming in this context, therefore, was to provide information that would encourage a more informed and dispassionate debate. The materials used were as follows:

(i) A short press-cutting printed on a worksheet which also gave general instructions for the task. This short report gave objective information about the likely change in the law, the organisations supporting it, and some outline information about the statistics relating to children's injuries in road accidents – 'Last year (1986), 89 per cent of children injured in road accidents were seated in the back and 91 per cent of those killed.' (See appendix C.)

(ii) When the discussions were under way and points were being made by the different groups from their own prior knowledge and experience, the teacher distributed a second off-print. This gave further newspaper reports of accidents in which seat-belts had either assisted or frustrated rescue attempts, or discussed problems associated with the proposed change in the law – parents with large families, for example, who would not have enough safety belts for every child, or the short journey made to school when cars were often fully loaded with children from different families.

(iii) After the discussion had been allowed to continue for a further phase, the teacher introduced another longer off-print from a magazine which provided a discussion of the main arguments in favour of wearing safety belts and some of the most common fears people express about their possible effects in an accident – being trapped by the belt, for example, especially in fire or water, or being injured because the belt fits badly.

As a result of the teacher's intervention in providing these materials, the discussion was perhaps excessively shaped and influenced by him. However, making the different off-prints available encouraged pupils to look beyond their own immediate experiences and assumptions and to take account of different kinds of evidence and perhaps conflicting points of view.

When off-prints or other resources are used to prime discussion in this way, they can obviously be provided at different points in the continuing debate, not at the beginning alone. Different sources of information can be introduced gradually, piece by piece, as discussion develops. Pupils are encouraged to pause in the debate, as they were in the example given, read an off-print and reflect on its contents, and then continue with the discussion, taking account of the different kinds of information provided.

Rules

We have emphasised how important it is for pupils to understand and accept classroom rules for group discussion. Many children, especially those from homes where the experience of extended discussion is rare, may at first find such rules alien and difficult to accept. The next example, therefore, is designed to help introduce a class to the procedures and self-control that are essential if further work in group discussion is to develop and thrive.

The context of the lesson to be described is a unit of work with a mixed-ability junior secondary class which led eventually to the completion of a piece of expressive, personal writing on the subject of 'Accidents' (serious or trivial). The main task was to be pupils' own accounts of some kind of accident that had happened to them. It could deal, for example, with a road accident, or with something that had happened at school or at home, or when they were with their friends.

They were to describe how the accident had come about, what actually happened, how they had felt, and what the final outcome was.

Before they began to write, though, there was to be a priming activity to help them recall events and decide how they were going to deal with the topic. They were to describe and discuss in their groups their recollected experiences on the subject, each concentrating on a particular event. The discussion could be about anything connected with the topic, but it was to take a very precise form. There were definite rules which they all had to abide by. First each group was to choose a chairperson. The boy or girl selected would be given a card on which the rules for the discussion were printed. At the end of the discussion the chairperson would report back to the rest of the class on how well their group had worked and on the difficulties they had encountered. To help them make these reports, when the discussions were over, every group member would fill in a short self-assessment questionnaire.

The rules printed on the discussion card were as follows:

(i) Each member of the group has to talk in turn for a maximum of two minutes on their chosen subject. The chairperson must strictly time this and indicate when the time is over.

(ii) While this person is talking, the rest of the group must be totally silent and must listen.

(iii) After each person has spoken, everyone in the group should ask one question in turn about what has been said. One question is the minimum expected of everyone in the group. You may ask more than one question, but the chairperson should make sure that no one asks too many.

(iv) The next person then speaks for two minutes and the process is repeated until everyone in the group has had a turn.

It is easy to react negatively and critically to these clearly defined rules. Some teachers have argued that, far from providing a supportive framework for pupils' discussions, the approach is more likely to create a strait-jacket. Many people feel, too, that being aware that you must speak for two minutes on a subject, even one you are confident you can handle, may provoke some anxiety. Similarly, knowing that you will have to ask a question after listening to another pupil's account may also be worrying for some. Children, normally fluent and garrulous, can be struck temporarily dumb by the experience. But these hostile arguments lose sight of the teacher's purposes in using the approach. The intention is not so much to promote and develop discussion skills in the classroom, as to establish the foundations that enable these skills to grow. The strategy is useful if you wish to introduce an enthusiastic, but undisciplined class, perhaps at the beginning of the school year, to the rules of group discussion. You want pupils to learn about the importance of turn-taking, listening carefully, asking one question at a time, and seeking to involve every member of the group in the debate. The approach also helps pupils to begin to comprehend the importance of developing skills in 'information-related' and 'extended' talk, which we discussed earlier, when they have to describe or explain something to others clearly and explicitly, and where they have to hold their listeners' attention for what may seem to them to be an eternity of time.

The final self-assessment questionnaire was short and to the point. Each pupil had to circle the appropriate answer to each of the following questions:

  (i) The most difficult part of the discussion for me was talking/ listening/answering a question.
 (ii) I think I was best at talking/listening/answering a question.
(iii) I found it easiest to talk/listen/ask a question.
(iv) When I had to talk, I felt relaxed/confident/nervous/ embarrassed/frightened.

In addition, they each had to fill in a grid indicating who (in their opinion) had talked a lot; who had talked little; who had said hardly anything; who listened well; who had not listened.

It is true the discussion appears to be less about the theme of 'Accidents' on which the class will eventually write, and more about learning the rules and procedures for group discussion. And in some ways the experiences provided by the lesson may have been frustrating and constraining for pupils eager to talk about what had actually happened to them. But for the teacher involved, the lesson was helping to form a foundation on which he could build for the rest of the school year and the lessons that were learned by the class on this occasion were ones to which he could later refer.

Case study: 'Ghost Hunting'

The classroom example which concludes this section is a case study of a young teacher at work with a first year mixed-ability class in an urban secondary school. The context of the lesson is a unit of work which explored (not too seriously) the theme of 'Ghosts and Apparitions'. Before the start of the lesson to be examined, there had already taken place a more formal whole-class discussion about pupils' own claimed experiences of supernatural events and the class had read and answered questions on an abridged version of the story 'The Canterville Ghost' by Oscar Wilde. The next important stage in the project was to be an extended writing task in which pupils would describe an imaginary night spent in a haunted house as 'ghost hunters'. The discursive lesson to be described would act as a preparation or form of priming for that task.

The lesson begins (perhaps predictably) with a short directive phase. The teacher first deals with initial classroom routines in settling the class after it has arrived in a state of some excitement from another distant part of the school and ensures coats are taken off. He reminds pupils about the theme of the unit and the work they have already completed. And finally he moves on to his main purpose in this phase – introducing and explaining the main topic for discussion.

He starts by reading to the class the following short passage while pupils listen:

'Things that go bump in the night' have a habit of instilling terror, so consider carefully before you go looking for spooks. They are shy, so prepare to be patient – hours can be spent watching a haunted room only to find that the phantom has taken a notion to materialise elsewhere. Like any good detective, a ghost hunter must start with the proper equipment. Certainly you need basic equipment that can be added to if you become hooked – as many of us are. The following is a basic list of what you will need:

(i)   an open and inquisitive mind
(ii)   a camera fitted with a flash and tripod
(iii)   a video camera
(iv)   a tape recorder
(v)   a thermometer – preferably a large one that can be read at a glance
(vi)   black nylon and cotton thread
(vii)   flour
(viii)   fingerprint detection kit.

He reads slowly and clearly and the pupils listen intently. The equipment list is already written on the blackboard and he reads through it again at a measured pace, pointing to the board as he reads. What pupils now have to do is discuss in groups the possible uses of the listed materials, if they were to go ghost hunting themselves. The note-taker in each group must keep a record of the different points they make.

The class at present is seated in pairs, partly according to friendships, and partly as a result of decisions taken by the teacher. To improve classroom control, he has deliberately seated some children close to the blackboard or his own desk, or has separated a particular child from a chosen partner. Pupils have designated groups for discussion with assigned roles in the group (leader and note-taker). The teacher now instructs the class to move quickly and quietly into their groups and begin work. The transition is made with some noise and confusion, but both are purposeful and easily contained.

The groups experience no problems in getting the discussion under way and most children have plenty to say. Children accept the conventions of the mode; individuals are prepared to listen as well as talk, the group leaders steer discussion along and take their groups through the agenda, and informal notes are kept. There is quite a lot of noise and some laughter. The children tackle the subject with considerable seriousness, though; it is obviously no joking matter to them. Most contributions seem to be thoughtful and sensible. The teacher moves round the groups, listening, asking questions and contributing. Pupils obviously accept his presence and like and respect him. When the noise level becomes too high, he intervenes clearly and firmly, using a hard, measured tone of voice to penetrate the noise and get the attention of the class. He waits for almost complete quiet and then speaks quietly himself. Pupils are warned to bring the noise level down while they are talking. The class at first responds. Discussion continues more quietly and then the noise level starts to rise again. The cycle of events is repeated.

When the teacher has judged that most groups are approaching or have reached the end of their agenda, he warns them that they will have to bring their discussions to a close. He then returns to the front of the class to make the transition to the final main phase of the lesson. He quietens the class and gains their attention. The groups are now to report back about the conclusions they have reached. Pupils remain in their places and the note-takers rather than the leaders are given responsibility for presenting each group's findings. The teacher works through the original list of essential requirements systematically and asks a different group for each answer.

There are problems in this phase. It is a difficult room for quiet speakers to be heard and the teacher has to ask for some answers to be repeated and has to relay other answers back to the whole class. Progress is therefore slow. None the less he is prepared to give time to ask pupils to develop their replies and he probes occasionally for more information when a reply is not completely clear. It emerges that most pupils believe that the equipment will be needed to distinguish between genuine ghosts and frauds. This phase of the lesson is obviously much more directive. Pupils have to put their hands up to ask a question or disagree, and they are willing to accept these rules. Time, however, runs out.

The teacher makes a hasty transition to the concluding phase of the lesson. He collects in the notes from the groups to look at them again before the next lesson. He moves pupils back to their original seats quickly and with some noise and good humoured chatter. As the lesson bell rings, he insists on everyone sitting silently, ready to leave. He then allows pupils to depart a row at a time, with the best behaved row going first. Altogether the lesson has lasted for 70 minutes – about 15 minutes for the introduction and explanation of the task, about 30 minutes for the discussion in groups, and about 20 minutes for the final plenary discussion.

Varied examples of classroom work implemented by different teachers have been provided in the preceding sections to illustrate some possible uses and interpretations of the discursive mode. If you wish to go on to examine critically and appraise your own classroom performance in discursive teaching (perhaps in collaboration with another colleague), figure 3.1 provides a checklist of questions for you to consider after you have taught an appropriate lesson or series of lessons in the mode. As with the previous checklist for directive teaching, this checklist should be used flexibly and is designed to help you to identify strengths and weaknesses in your own classroom performance.

Checklist of skills – the discursive mode

THE DISCURSIVE MODE OF TEACHING

Planning the lesson
Was the topic chosen for this class appropriate?
Was the task defined and structured clearly enough?
How successful was any selected stimulus or catalyst to the discussion?
Were the size and composition of the groups appropriate?

Implementing the lesson
Was there sufficient 'priming' before or during the discussion?
Did pupils have enough time to complete the task(s)?
How successful was I in restraining my own contribution to the discussion?
Was my presence supportive or inhibiting to pupils?
Was there adequate feedback to pupils at the end of the lesson?

Managing the classroom
Were the pupils seated appropriately for this mode?
How successful was I in making transitions between the different phases of the lesson?
Was I successful in monitoring the progress and behaviour of all the groups?
Did the pupils accept the rules and procedures appropriate to this mode?

Evaluating success
Were the pupils interested in the lesson? Did they all co-operate and participate?
Who talked most? Were some pupils merely silent listeners?
Was the content of each discussion relevant to the topic set?
Can I comment on the achievements of individual speakers as a result of the lesson?

Figure 3.1

Chapter four

Solving problems

The discursive mode of teaching, it has been argued, will inevitably include an element of directive control in the way a teacher sets up and organises a classroom discussion. However, once pupils begin to participate in the discussion, especially when it is arranged in small groups, they clearly are allowed a much greater measure of freedom and responsibility to pace and develop the lesson than is the case in traditional directive teaching. They are more likely to be actively involved in the lesson and will have more opportunities to participate in it. The inquiry mode, which is the next model of teaching and learning to be examined, continues further the devolution of responsibility from teacher to pupils and allows a class much greater freedom in deciding on the content and progress of an individual lesson or a unit of classroom work.

The characteristics of the inquiry mode

Inquiry teaching is founded on the premiss that children are by nature inquisitive beings. From the earliest stages in their development they intuitively create and test out their own hypotheses. They learn by trial and error and begin to ask their own questions in their attempts to make sense of the environment they inhabit. It should, therefore, be the aim of the school, so the argument goes, to harness this potential source of energy so that the classroom can become a purposeful context for individual learning. Far from being passive recipients of received knowledge, pupils should be encouraged to construct their own knowledge and understanding and develop for themselves essential personal and mechanical skills. The teacher's role is not to transmit information, but to be engaged whenever possible in the processes of learning alongside the pupil, acting as a guide and a resource, as the child experiences some of the excitement and satisfaction of personal discovery.

As I argued in the opening chapter, it is difficult, if not impossible, for any teacher working today within the framework of compulsory schooling, with its demands for teacher accountability and clearly defined, visible outcomes, to carry this model of teaching and learning to its logical extreme. This extreme position would allow pupils the freedom to set their own agenda for classroom work, to organise and pace it themselves week by week, and to select styles of learning that seemed appropriate to their own recognised needs. None the less, it is still feasible to offer pupils more choice and greater participation in classroom activities than is often the case, and to give them increased responsibilities for deciding what they are to learn and how they can best learn it. And this can be done without losing sight of the realities of school and classroom and the pressures under which teachers work.

What would a typical lesson be like, then, if this mode of teaching were to be implemented in, for example, a junior secondary classroom? First, the initial phase of the lesson would almost certainly be quite different from the examples of directive and discursive lessons already studied. There would probably be no introductory directive phase at all. Pupils would enter the classroom probably gradually in small groups rather than *en masse* as a whole class. The classroom is likely to be set out with desks arranged in groups with pupils facing each other, rather than in ranks facing the teacher or blackboard. There would be a variety of resources in the room, especially books, materials and perhaps some pieces of equipment like overhead projector, tape recorder and microcomputer. The teacher would be present in the room to receive pupils and this classroom would be her base where virtually all of her teaching takes place. There could be occasional comments or questions from teacher to individual pupils or vice-versa as the class entered the room, but pupils would show that they accepted that their first important task was to organise themselves for the coming lesson. They might bring their work to the room with them, but it is more likely that they would have to go to a shelf or cupboard to collect their folders of work. They would sit down in their accustomed places and either begin work on a new task or continue with the work of the previous lesson. This initial phase of the lesson when pupils organised themselves for work would happen with some noise and chatter, but it would proceed smoothly and with little intervention from the teacher.

It is likely that the class would be engaged in a variety of different tasks organised under the heading of a theme – 'My World', for example. This theme would have been selected by the teacher or possibly by the class itself. At the outset of the project pupils would have been given a worksheet which gave detailed information about the range of tasks that it is possible for them to complete. Again, these tasks might be created and compiled by the teacher or from suggestions made by members of the class. These tasks may require pupils to write expressively and imaginatively about aspects of their home, family and friends, or about their own dreams and hopes for the future. Or pupils might be asked to research some aspects of their community and present the information they compile in the form of a booklet for an interested visitor. The worksheet could also direct pupils to particular classroom texts or other resource materials in order to read poems or short stories connected with the theme and complete associated written exercises. If the class is a randomly grouped, mixed-ability class, it is possible that some tasks will be graded according to their assumed level of difficulty. In this way everyone in the class appears to be working in much the same way and on similar activities, whereas in reality some tasks are adjusted to cater for different needs and levels of achievement. Similarly the teacher may have different expectations about the amount of work it is reasonable for each pupil to complete, with some children expected to produce a lot of written work and others comparatively little. And it would be possible for some pupils to listen to a story being read on audio-tape by means of a listening junction box and tape recorder rather than read it for themselves without support.

Pupils would take pride in the way their work was presented. Their folders would be attractively decorated and there would probably be a separate title page with the heading 'My World'. The pages of hand-writing would be illustrated with photographs and pictures cut out from magazines and have coloured headings. As the lesson progressed, it would become clear that pupils were either working individually or in pairs or small teams. The range of simultaneous activities in the class would be varied. Occasionally a pupil would get up and move to another part of the room to consult a text or another pupil, to take a coloured pen from the teacher's desk, or sharpen a pencil. Possibly two children collaborating on a task would ask the teacher for permission to go to the main school library for further research. In one corner of the room a small group of pupils might be listening to a tape, another pair might be using the microcomputer as a word processor to type up a magazine article about their neighbourhood. Some children would be writing, others reading, or discussing how to answer a particular set of questions related to a text.

Throughout the lesson the teacher would move from group to group or from individual to individual, checking that progress was being made, answering any questions or making suggestions about the best way forward for that particular child. It is likely that pupils would also be deliberately consulting her, asking for a clearer explanation of some-thing on the worksheet or seeking help and advice. Occasionally, as in the discursive mode, she would intervene firmly and authoritatively either to remind pupils about some aspect of the project that they seemed

61

to be overlooking or warning them about the level of noise. Probably just before the end of the lesson she would warn the class that it would have to bring its work to a conclusion. Perhaps the lesson would be stopped by the ringing of the interval bell. Children would move about the classroom, returning books and materials to their correct places, and returning their own files and folders to the cupboard where they are stored. Some pupils may continue to work because they particularly want to get something finished and in order to do so they may be prepared to take time from their interval break. The remaining members of the class will gradually disperse in much the same way that they had entered the classroom for the start of the lesson. The teacher meanwhile has to reorganise herself and prepare for the next incoming class.

The description makes devising and managing the lesson sound deceptively simple and straightforward. And, of course, in the hands of an experienced and skilled practitioner, the lesson also *looks* effortless from the viewpoint of an outsider or a beginning teacher. It is only when you attempt to implement a unit of work yourself with a class that is unaccustomed to working in this way that you begin to realise how difficult it is to master the necessary skills and professional understanding that underpin this mode of teaching.

What, then, are the professional skills you will need to acquire yourself if you are to use the mode successfully? And what will your pupils need to understand and accept both about the procedures and rules that will operate in your classroom and about their own roles as learners?

The skills of inquiry teaching

Careful planning and lesson preparation are particularly important for beginning or inexperienced teachers. You should not be surprised, though, if more experienced colleagues sometimes cynically claim that they never prepare work themselves and that all their major decisions about a lesson are taken (at best) on the journey from staff base to classroom. Usually, experienced teachers underestimate two important dimensions to the problem. The first is the psychological importance of planning to the beginning teacher. Careful preparation helps to build up your confidence as you approach a possible confrontation with a class; you need the security which comes from knowing what it is you plan to do.

The second dimension which is often unrecognised is the wealth of experience that teachers store in their own heads. They possess there a complex resource bank that they can readily draw on for instant decisions and action. This resource obviously includes ideas for lessons, and possible texts and materials derived from earlier classroom activities, but, just as important, it holds the recollected experiences which have been assembled as a result of teaching countless pupils and classes. It holds advice not only about what to teach, but how to teach it, about how to respond to individual behaviour problems, and how to manage and control a class. It helps to create expectations about, for example, what a first year class will be like, what will interest and what will bore them, how to pitch the level of difficulty, and what to anticipate in the way of work and behaviour.

In inquiry teaching careful and effective planning may well be crucial to success. The earlier description of a hypothetical lesson in this mode showed how complex the management of classroom activities can be, with children working on a variety of tasks in different ways and at different speeds. Unless these activities are built on a foundation of careful preparation, this complexity can easily become confusion. Before beginning a lesson or sequence of lessons, you have to think through carefully what tasks should be available to pupils, which (if any) of them should be 'core' activities to be completed by everyone, and which tasks should remain optional. You will also have to try to anticipate what will be essential and desirable in the way of classroom texts, materials and equipment, and what role will be played by other sources of support (like the library).

In fact, before taking on the full demands of the mode, as it has been described, and attempting to implement an extended unit of work, it may be advisable to allow yourself time to develop your expertise and confidence and to seek to introduce aspects of the mode gradually into your teaching. Consequently the discussion and exemplification that follow will encourage you to test out an inquiry approach to teaching initially in a limited and controlled way so that the skills implicit in this mode will eventually, with experience, become an accepted part of your own bank of professional resources.

Intrinsic motivation is an essential ingredient in the success of the inquiry mode. Pupils must be interested in the organising themes that underpin a unit of classroom work and they must wish to explore the topics the teacher makes available to them. It is likely, therefore, that the themes or subjects you select will be close to pupils' lives and immediate concerns. Similarly, any texts you decide to use will be written in way that pupils find accessible and within their capabilities as readers. Materials you create yourself will also need to be attractively produced and clearly presented. Children are obviously accustomed in their lives outside of school to using a wide range of attractive consumer products; they are critical of shoddy packaging. Commercially produced textbooks are now mostly attractive, clearly presented and colourful, with excellent photographs and line illustrations.

It may not be easy to produce in-school materials to match these standards, but you should (and with modern technology you can) at least try. You can set out your own material clearly and attractively. It may be economical to compress as much copy as possible on to a single sheet of paper, but such a wall of print does not encourage even a skilled reader to give attention to the information you are trying to communicate. 'White space' on the page helps to make a worksheet more accessible and readable. And you can further lighten the effect by the use of drawings, cartoons and line designs. Your initial aim is to be eye-catching; you wish to interest your audience in the materials you offer. Many worksheets and materials produced by teachers have quite the opposite effect. They present pupils with a mass of print, are often handwritten and difficult to decipher, and present nothing to catch the eye or entertain the reader.

Positive motivation is achieved, though, much more by the nature of the tasks you devise than by the quality of the packaging you offer. In preparing tasks, you have to think in terms of an investigation pupils will carry out, a topic to be explored, or, most especially, a problem that will have to be solved. Despite the exemplification provided so far, complexity in classroom management and diversity in the tasks offered are not essential features in an inquiry approach. To give yourself time to develop your confidence and skills, you can devise a task that must be completed by the whole class, or a series of tasks which involve one or more features of the mode. For example, the unit of work that gave rise to the close study of 'Welsh Incident', described at the conclusion of chapter two, also involved pupils in solving the problem of how to escape from the imaginary Castle Krill. The class was given a plan of the castle's rooms, passageways and dungeons; pupils knew the circumstances in which the characters in the story were trapped there and the dangers they had to overcome. In groups they had to work out how they could escape.

The importance of pupils understanding and accepting the procedures and rules for classroom discussion was emphasised in the last chapter. A similar understanding and acceptance of the rules and procedures appropriate to an inquiry approach are equally important if this mode is to succeed. Pupils must recognise that the main responsibility for proceeding with a task or a scheme of work is theirs. The resources will be available, together with any guidelines and support provided by the teacher, but it will be up to the pupils to organise and manage the time that is available to complete the tasks as best they can. It will be for them (or possibly initially the teacher) to decide whether they work as individuals, or co-operatively in pairs or small groups. If they decide to work co-operatively, they must accept shared responsibility for completing the work set, learn to work as part of a team, and be prepared to delegate particular tasks to individuals, if necessary. As with the management of group discussions in class, the teacher's willingness to set clear targets to aim for and deadlines to meet can provide an additional sense of urgency and purpose.

The class must also be prepared to accept that, as in a discussion, the amount of noise it produces must be limited and controlled and pupils will expect the teacher to take appropriate action if an acceptable threshold is passed. Pupils will have to learn that movement about the classroom by individuals is permissible for certain purposes, but that movement by pairs or groups of pupils at the same time is less acceptable because of the noise and distraction it creates. Leaving the classroom will almost certainly require the teacher's permission; you need to know where pupils are going, what the purpose of the excursion is, and how long they are likely to be. Again, these rules and procedures need to be made clear and explicit to pupils before any work can begin.

Once work is planned and under way in the classroom, an essential skill for the teacher to acquire is the ability to manage the development of the lesson and monitor pupils' behaviour and progress as it unfolds. If the the procedures for the mode have been conveyed clearly and are accepted by pupils, the actual management of time and the development of the lesson will probably be less important than in directive or discursive teaching. In an inquiry lesson you are more likely to be 'reactive' than 'proactive'. That is, you are more likely to react to pupils' difficulties and their behaviour, helping them to make progress with the activities of the lesson and ensuring that they remain 'on task'. You are less likely to look ahead and anticipate possible problems with the development of the lesson, making as a result impromptu changes to your plans.

In inquiry teaching the lesson should move ahead as a result of its own momentum and pupils' involvement in the activities. To be realistic, though, you will almost certainly need to keep alert, as when monitoring progress and behaviour in the discursive mode. While you are involved in the process of giving help to an individual or group, you will still need to keep the rest of the class under surveillance and be prepared to intervene, if work is not proceeding smoothly. You will have to keep track of what individuals or groups have achieved in a lesson and of the progress they are making through a longer unit of work. As I argued in the opening chapter, the demands on your time and expertise will inevitably increase and the level of stress will rise as you seek to implement more complicated schemes of work and make available to pupils a more varied range of topics and tasks. Above all, it will become increasingly difficult for you to keep account of what individual children have achieved and the progress they have made over an extended period of time. And this will be especially true if children have spent much of their time working as members of a team.

When you decide to adopt an inquiry approach in your classroom, then, you must be prepared to commit additional time and energy to planning and preparing lessons. Almost certainly, too, you will have to work hard to establish the rules and procedures for the smooth running of the mode in your classroom. And assessing and monitoring pupils' progress are likely to prove complex and demanding. On the other hand, most teachers who use the mode effectively seem to agree that the actual experience of the mode in the classroom is relaxing and satisfying for the teacher. The climate for learning is usually positive and often informal. There is little sense of confrontation between teacher and taught and relationships are often easy and good humoured.

From the pupil's point of view, it is also easy to see why the mode is well liked. The teacher is obviously at pains to gain your interest. She tries to present work attractively and you are often offered a variety of tasks to choose from. There is the opportunity to explore subjects that are of interest and personal relevance to you, and to work co-operatively as a member of a team. Classroom rules exist, but they are more flexible and open than in a directive classroom. You are allowed greater freedom to move about the room and even to escape from it altogether on occasions. And above all, you can work at your own pace and in a way that seems to suit you. You are permitted to talk 'on the job' and the teacher will not put undue pressure on you to finish a piece of work at the same time as everyone else in the class or to cover the same ground.

Perhaps, though, we should end on a note of caution, if we are to present a balanced and objective view of the mode. There are weaknesses as well as strengths, disadvantages as well as advantages. And from the pupil's point of view, the mode does also offer a tempting opportunity to avoid undue pressure and hard work. If you are allowed the freedom and responsibility to pace yourself in a lesson or unit of work, it will probably always prove attractive to some children to move as slowly as possible. When you are given the opportunity to move about the classroom, it is tempting to use it to waste time and distract others. If you are offered a menu of possible activities, it is tempting to choose only those that you know you can cope with, not to select any task that is a little difficult or challenging. And if you work as a member of a team, it can be tempting, too, to allow others to do most of the work and remain a silent and uncomplaining fellow traveller yourself.

It is sometimes all too easy for even a skilled and experienced teacher to miss such pupils; they often merge into the little-recognised grey areas of a class. And when such pupils are well known to teachers as difficult and potentially troublesome individuals, it is equally tempting to overlook their behaviour. In order to keep the work and routines of your classroom running smoothly, it often appears pragmatic to adopt an 'avoidance of provocation' strategy. You will almost certainly feel a sense of guilt if you allow these more troublesome pupils to remain quiet but relatively inactive in your lessons, but experienced teachers will argue that the interests of the majority in the class are at stake. If you decide to give additional time and effort to the individuals concerned to ensure that they are purposefully engaged, the rest of the class may well suffer as a result. (See Hargreaves, Hester, and Mellor 1975: 239–45).

Talking and learning

In a discursive lesson the central focus of activity for pupils is talking and listening. As we indicated in the previous chapter, in these circumstances the creation of a comparatively high volume of noise in the classroom is inevitable. In the inquiry mode, on the other hand, the central focus of activity is likely to be the attempted solution of some kind of problem or the investigation of a topic or issue. In this context some pupils may well choose to work as individuals, but most seem to prefer to work co-operatively in pairs or small groups. As they begin to make progress with the task, again, almost inevitably, they will talk, perhaps to themselves, as they struggle to make sense of something or give themselves instructions to follow, and almost certainly to each other, as members of a group interact. In terms of management and control, as teacher, you may again perceive this talk as a source of potential distraction and as a threat to your own authority. It may be a feature of the lesson that you feel you have to accept grudgingly because it is inevitable that children will talk when they work together in this way, but deeper intuitions warn you that you should discourage it, because the noise it creates may present a poor image of your classroom control to an outsider. Should they be making quite so much noise? Can this amount of noise really be productive and purposeful?

As with the discursive mode, both you and the class have to accept that the level of classroom noise that is created must be kept within reasonable bounds. But it is equally important to accept that pupils talking 'on the job' is an integral part of inquiry teaching. It should be encouraged and valued because it makes an often unrecognised contribution to the processes of learning. If, for example, pupils choose to work co-operatively in pairs or small groups, they are likely to attempt to work together to produce some kind of outcome rather than be prepared to accept a simple imposed solution. In a single class of pupils the interpersonal dynamics of each group will inevitably differ. In one group, for example, a clear leader may emerge, more directive and assertive than the rest. The climate within another group, on the other hand, may be more open and democratic with shared decisions being taken. A third group may be more authoritarian in style, with the more forceful member(s) of the group imposing decisions and conclusions on the rest who seem content to be more subservient and passive. However, whatever the mixture of personalities that comprise each group and the system of social control it intuitively adopts, as teacher, you must expect and encourage a lively and purposeful interchange of views and opinions as the groups work. Within the context of the inquiry mode, pupils are continuing to learn how to discuss, how to express themselves orally, and how to listen intelligently. This is an essential component of the procedures, expectations and rules of inquiry teaching. And it is again important for you to communicate these expectations clearly and explicitly.

Obviously we can and do learn by listening. And pupils often seem to learn from each other at least as effectively as from the teacher. If, as a pupil, you are seeking to solve some kind of problem set by the teacher and you are working as a member of a team, you should be prepared to listen to and evaluate what others have to say. How relevant are their contributions? How useful are they as a step towards solving the problem? You may well have ideas of your own, but you should be prepared to listen none the less, and you may well find that you will adapt or develop your own thinking in response to what you hear.

Just as importantly, though, you, the pupil, will want to contribute your own thoughts to the group's endeavours. And in seeking to do this, you will almost certainly be helping to develop further your skills and self-confidence in oral expression. In some circumstances, you may find that the words stubbornly refuse to come, or come only hesitantly and falteringly. And you may be faced with the dilemma of not knowing what it is you think about a subject, until you hear what you actually say – a problem that seems to be very real for many children. And it is here that the real importance of encouraging talk in inquiry teaching lies. You should not expect conversation to flow readily and easily from speaker to speaker. In this context pupils should not be engaged merely in informal, interpersonal chat. If they are engrossed in a problem or an issue, you should expect the talk to be disjointed, perhaps hesitant, and sometimes incoherent. Pupils are likely to be talking their way, perhaps slowly and with difficulty, towards a possible resolution of a problem.

To sum up, then: if you are a pupil, it is important for you to talk in this kind of problem-solving context, not merely because it will help you to develop your oral skills and increase your self-confidence (although these goals are both important), nor because it will give others the opportunity to learn from you (which is important, too). It is essential because it helps you to learn yourself. You will be struggling to express and organise ideas that are only partially formed and recognised within your own head. By articulating them, you not only give your thoughts a kind of existence, but you also begin to give them a semblance of shape and form. You gradually become more aware of what you think, feel and understand and of how your ideas interconnect and interrelate. The process is assisted and encouraged as you are made to feel the need to communicate your ideas to others and defend and explain further what it is you are trying to say.

Consider, for example the following short extract. A class of 11 year olds have listened to the opening of a ghost story read to them by their teacher. In it a man has accepted a challenge to spend a night alone in a room that is said to be haunted. As he prepares for bed, he begins to feel more and more nervous and checks the room thoroughly for any trace of anything suspicious. At last he is satisfied that the room is safe and he goes to bed 'exhausted but happy'. In groups pupils have to decide for themselves what the outcome of the story will be – will the man be troubled by a ghost? Will he be tricked by his friends, or what will happen?

There are four boys and two girls in the group to be studied and the teacher is not present as they talk. Simon is acting as chairman. The discussion (which was recorded on audio-tape) is noisy, excited and good humoured:

Simon: Right, Lindsay. We'll go round again. Do you think it's a ghost or a man tricking him?

Lindsay: A man tricking him. Well, not a man tricking him, just something tricking him.

Simon: [To Clare] What do you think?

Clare: I agree with John.

Simon: And what's that?

Clare: ...about toads, these wee things...

Simon: Toads?...Animals then? You go for animals? Or a man?

Clare: Aye...mmm [not clear]

Simon: [To Stuart] What do you go for?

Stuart: I just say it's sort of...death-watch beetles or something, and they're under the floorboards ticking an' that.

Simon: I don't think it would be that intricate, Stuart. Could death-watch beetles...?

Stuart: [in background] Yea, well, it's an old house, in'it?...an' that's a ghost place...it's supposed to be...

Simon: Tommy, what do you think?

Tommy: I think it's a...it's a ghost.

Simon: I agree with you, Tommy.

Clare: They could have a loft.

Tommy: It's not called a ghost...it's not called a ghost story for nothing.

Stuart: [tapping] But it says he tapped all over the floor for... [general babble]

John: I've got a ghost book at home full of ghost stories an' all, but out of five ghost stories, only a couple 've got anything about ghosts. The other ones have got some unnatural phen[omenon].

Stuart: Aaaah! [mimicking]

Simon: Yea, but it's an old hou...

Linda: John, there could be a loft. He never went up into the loft, did he?

John: Well, I don't know. There might not 've been one. It doesn't tell you.

Linda: I know, but there could have been.

John: He looked everwhere, it said.

Simon: Look, it didn't tell you a lot of things. It didn't tell you what colour his pyjamas were or anything...

John: There could be a million things...[background noise...colour of pyjamas...] be bats... there could be bats...you get millions of them in old haunted rooms...and there'll obviously be millions of bats...be millions of frogs...be millions of mice...rats...there'd be everything.

Stuart: No' millions.

Lindsay: I mean...I mean, if it's an ol' house...

Simon: Nobody thinks it'll be a man now?

Tommy: [to John] You've never seen a rat, son...you've never seen the size of one. They're aboot that size [gesture]...

Lindsay: I don't think rats could get through a wee spa...a wee thing like that.

John: But they could have a rat hole.

Tommy: Toads are big enough. Toads are about that size.

Clare: In from behind the wardrobe...[babble...yes, his friends'll try to trick him...] have a wee hole behind the wardrobe....So...

John: He moves the wardrobe...[babble...it could be the door he moved...the chair behind it...]

Simon: Right, I think...I think I agree with Stuart, Lindsay, and Clare and John. It'll be an animal...or something funny.

Tommy: I don't get it...I don't agree...and I'm no' gonnae change. I don't agree, 'cos how could you get an animal in there? ...

There is a sense of excitement and headlong momentum in the exchanges and little apparent evidence of hesitancy (especially when the discussion is heard rather than read). Occasionally the enthusiasm of the group hinders progress, despite the endeavours of the chairman to control their energy. But closer examination of the transcript shows that some children are clearly less confident and more restrained than others (Lindsay, for example). Above all, we can observe how different children test out their ideas, listen to and evaluate the contributions of others, and think rapidly and creatively. The language they use tends to be abrupt and disjointed and it is sometimes difficult to grasp the logic of the progress that is being made. What they have to say sometimes remains unfinished, they make false starts, they interrupt, they repeat themselves and they appeal to each other for support and for evidence. Perhaps, if the teacher had been present throughout, the group might have been more orderly and subdued. But in these circumstances much of the spontaneity and perhaps the value of the discussion might also have been lost. (The same transcript is discussed in Northcroft 1984: 38.)

Planning and presenting inquiry lessons

Like discursive lessons, an inquiry approach can be applied to any aspect of the English curriculum and used with classes of any age and level of achievement. It can involve responses to a text or the investigation of some kind of problem or issue related to a topic or theme. The examples that follow are again taken from the classroom work of both experienced and inexperienced teachers, and, as with exemplification in other modes, they are intended to show how the characteristic features of inquiry teaching come alive in the reality of a classroom. The examples will also illustrate some of the professional skills that are essential if the mode is to be used successfully.

If you wish to test out the approach in your own classroom, it is advisable (as I argued earlier) to try to limit the demands you have to meet in terms of preparation and classroom management, and to keep your approach as simple as possible. Consequently, the classroom examples described and discussed show a teacher working on one task only, with the whole class, rather than a more complicated approach in which different groups of pupils would be working on a number of tasks at different speeds and possibly in different ways.

Using a text

One of the legacies of traditional directive teaching is a possible lack of confidence on the part of pupils in talking about their own responses to the experience of reading a literary text. Traditionally, the teacher is regarded as the most important source of knowledge and understanding available to the class. If, for example, as a senior pupil you have been reading a novel or play as part of your English course, it is easy to assume, especially if the course leads to some kind of external examination, that your role is to listen to and note the responses of the teacher and to attempt to reproduce these responses in any discussion or writing task that you are set. And, as we showed in the earlier discussion of the directive mode, there is an important element of truth in such an assumption. The teacher can and should act as a model who helps a class to understand better how a sophisticated, expert reader behaves, the kinds of questions you should ask and the kinds of responses that might be appropriate.

At the same time, though, as I have already argued, it is possible (and desirable) to give pupils more freedom and responsibility to explore the meanings of texts for themselves. Many teachers discover, for example, how successful and stimulating it often proves, especially with senior classes, when you admit to a class that you have been struggling yourself with the meaning of a particular poem or part of a text that is being studied in detail, and that you are baffled by it. What does it mean? What is the poet trying to communicate? Can the class help? Genuine discussion follows in an attempt to solve the problem, and different interpretations are put forward and considered. Ideas are tested out against the evidence of the text itself and possible solutions begin to emerge and strengthen or fade. However, although this admission of non-comprehension (feigned or real) on the part of the teacher can prove to be an effective and rewarding strategy, unfortunately it is not one that you can exploit too much. Inevitably, excessive use tends to destroy your authority and credibility as a teacher, and pupils' confidence in you.

Alternatively, pupils can be given a copy of an unseen text (a poem by a set author, for example) which has had key words or images deleted. Working in pairs or groups, they are then asked to suggest and discuss possible appropriate words to fill the blanks and to provide reasons for their choices. Finally the groups compare their own choices with the original complete text, possibly in a teacher-led plenary discussion.

Another problem-solving strategy involves older pupils tracing a theme or literary technique through a series of selected poems or short stories that they have already studied in isolation. The teacher selects an appropriate theme or technique ('The Importance of the Individual', or the use of figurative language, for example) and asks the class, again working in pairs or groups, to trace and comment on the theme or technique as it emerges from their re-reading and discussion of the texts concerned. Again there can be a final reporting back phase when each group presents its findings for further discussion (Scottish Consultative Council on the Curriculum 1989: 14–21).

Although there are obviously many possible ways of approaching a text using the inquiry mode, the most common form of problem-solving task in this field in the classroom usually involves some kind of textual reconstruction – that is, a text is not presented to a class in its normal published form. Instead it is altered or reorganised in some way. Textual reconstruction can include the following three distinctive strategies:

(i) deletion of random or key words (as in the example given above);

(ii)   the re-sequencing of 'scrambled' paragraphs into the correct or 'best' order;

(iii)   predicting the possible developments in the unfolding of a narrative as pupils are gradually provided with more and more information from episodes in a (correctly sequenced) text.

These techniques are discussed and illustrated at length elsewhere (see, for example, Lunzer and Gardner 1979: chapter 9) and are now widely used in schools. What follows, therefore, is a single example of how one reading sequencing exercise was prepared and implemented by an experienced teacher in a particular classroom.

The text chosen was a short story written by a 13-year-old boy, a former pupil of the teacher. It is called 'The Werewolf Strikes Again' and it describes how a group of scouts at week-end camp go into the local town on Saturday night to see the film which gives the story its title. As the boys make their way back to the camp in the dark, through a cemetery and across fields, various frightening events occur, some humorous, others more disturbing and difficult to explain. It is an entertaining story, which is well told (see appendix D).

The text was typed out without alteration and divided into eleven 'chunks', each about eight lines long (with breaks at the end of a section). Each chunk was clearly divided from the rest of the text on the master copy by a ruled line and alphabetically labelled. The alphabetical labelling, however, did not correspond to the story's narrative sequence; the first two chunks of text, for example, were labelled E and H and the final section F. The story was photocopied in this form to provide multiple copies for the class. Then the pages were guillotined along the ruled lines to separate the text of the story into the different segments. These segments or chunks of text were then scrambled so that they did not correspond to the correct sequence of events. In other words, each pupil would have a copy of the complete story, but it would be cut up into segments and the segments would be arranged in an incoherent and confused sequence. The story was ready for classroom use in this form – fifteen bundles of guillotined scrambled text, with each bundle held together by a paper clip, enough copies for one text between two pupils.

In the lesson itself the class of 11-year-olds (of varied abilities and levels of achievement) was organised to work in pairs. Each pair was given one copy only of the bundled text as sharing the material encourages pupils to work co-operatively and discuss the task. They were told to unpin the bundle and lay the pieces out on the desks before them in the correct alphabetical order. This they did. The teacher then explained that what they had before them was a complete story, but although the pieces were arranged in the correct alphabetical order, this was not the correct order of events in the story. The task that faced them was a kind of reading jigsaw puzzle. What they had to do was to read the different pieces of text and decide together how the pieces of the story fitted together. What did they think was the correct order of events in the story? They could examine and read the pieces in any order, they could think and talk about the problem, but they had to be able to justify (to the teacher and the rest of the class) the order of events they finally decided on. They would have about 20 minutes to do this.

After this directive introduction to explain the nature of the task, the pupils began work. Initially they started quietly, with most pupils reading, but soon the noise level rose as they began to talk about how the story was likely to begin and develop. They began to move the pieces of text about on the desks, trying out different possible orders. Some took the metaphor of the jigsaw puzzle literally, and unsuccessfully attempted to match the edges of the segments as a short-cut to the solution. Others appeared to concentrate on reading first and last lines of segments in the hope that they would find an obvious connection. Whatever strategy pupils decided to use, the task was obviously motivating; the momentum of the lesson was maintained and interest did not appear to flag. While the pairs worked noisily, the teacher moved quietly from group to group, listening and watching. At an early point he sat down with one pair of pupils who were experiencing difficulty in making any headway and helped them to decide what the first unit of the sequence should be.

After about 15 minutes some pairs were beginning to claim that they had finished, so the teacher interrupted work to get the attention of the whole class. If they thought they had finished, they were to read through the story carefully from beginning to end and check that it made good sense. Work then continued and the teacher moved round the class checking to see if a pair's order of events corresponded to the author's original order. In many cases it did not, and so the pair was told to look again at the decisions they had made, often with reference to a particular part of the story.

After about 20 minutes the teacher told the class that they must finish what they were doing and he stopped them soon afterwards. Their next job was to check that the order of events they had decided on matched the author's own order. First the teacher read out slowly the correct alphabetical sequence of sections – E, H, A, etc. Then he asked how many members of the class had themselves decided on that order. Only about three pairs had, although some pairs had not had enough time to complete the task. Next, the class was told to rearrange the segments of the story on their desks in the author's sequence, if they hadn't already done so, and, as they did this, the teacher repeated the correct alphabetical order of the segments.

Finally he read the whole piece aloud so that they had a clear idea of the story the author had intended to tell. When the reading was over, a lively discussion followed, led by the teacher and with a number of pupils contributing, about what had actually happened to the boys in the story. Some pupils were obviously not convinced that the author's order of events was as good as their own, but most seemed to understand the story better as a result of the exercise. The teacher concluded the discussion by asking what they thought the title of the story should be, as this had not been included in the text given to the class.

This final phase of the lesson was brought to an end by the teacher about five minutes before the interval bell. He ensured that the slips of paper were put together in the correct alphabetical order by pupils and paper-clipped together. They were then collected and placed in a box for future use. In all, the lesson had lasted for about 40 minutes.

The lesson was clearly successful. Pupils enjoyed the story and found its style and content accessible, but in no way patronising. They clearly enjoyed working on the sequencing exercise and worked hard, noisily, and with good humour. Again, when events are described in this way, the management and control of the lesson appear to be deceptively easy and smooth. In fact, the success of the lesson was built on considerable hard work and skill. For example, the actual preparation of the materials obviously took time and care. The class was also accustomed to working in this way; they accepted the rules and procedures of the mode and the overall authority of the teacher in the classroom was never in doubt. The teacher himself was clear and business-like at the beginning of the lesson, explaining the nature of the task and what had to be achieved in the time allocated. The management of giving out the bundles of text and getting the pieces arranged on the desks was arranged confidently and quickly. The transitions between the different phases of the lesson were negotiated smoothly and authoritatively and the management of the conclusion was also quick and efficient.

Simulation

The second classroom example to be described and discussed is quite different. It is taken from a unit of work with a class of 14-year-olds on the theme of holidays. The class was 'banded' as a group of average achievers and the teacher involved in the lesson was much less experienced than the teacher in the previous example.

The unit had begun with lessons exploring possible problems in choosing and booking a holiday. For the first lesson the teacher had devised a collection of simulated advertisements for hotels and guest houses and separate descriptions of contrasting families. Working in groups of about four, pupils had had to examine this information and attempt to decide which hotel or guest house would be best suited to the needs of particular families.

In the next lesson pupils were given the task of making a simulated telephone call to a travel agent to book a selected holiday. Pupils worked in pairs guided by a worksheet prepared by the teacher (see appendix E). The worksheet required each group to make three main decisions:

(i)   the creation of an imaginary family with names, interests and ages;

(ii) the nature of the holiday they wanted to book – for example, seaside, scenic, or activity-centred;

(iii) the questions they wished to ask before making a firm booking – for example, seasonal changes in prices, possible concessions for families, the facilities offered by the hotel.

After discussing and completing the worksheet, the pairs first rehearsed their telephone conversations where they sat, with one pupil acting as caller and the other as travel agent, and then pairs were selected at random to perform the calls in front of the class. After each performance further questions were asked and suggestions made by both teacher and pupils.

The subsequent lesson is the one to be examined in more detail. This dealt with the aftermath of an unsuccessful holiday and a letter of complaint sent to a travel agent by a dissatisfied customer. In the first phase of the lesson, after settling the class and quietening them, the teacher briefly reminded pupils about progress to date on the theme, and then gave out copies of a new worksheet to every member of the class (see appendix E). The worksheet was headed 'Wish You Were Here?' and comprised three parts:

(i)   a short description of the imaginary 'Hotel Paloma Blanca', giving details (as though in a travel brochure) of its situation and amenities;

(ii) a letter of complaint to the 'Happy Holiday Company' written by a Mr Fred Smith detailing his reasons for his dissatisfaction with a recent holiday at the hotel; he claimed that the firm's brochure gave a false view of what the hotel was like and requested compensation for the discomfort he and his family had suffered;

(iii) details of the task that each group would have to complete.

The final task took the following form. Each group had to imagine that they represented, not Mr Smith, but the managing board of the firm of travel agents. In this role, they then had to examine Mr Smith's letter and decide how many of his complaints were the responsibility of their own travel firm; how many were the fault of the hotel and beyond the firm's control; how many were outside anyone's control and were the result of bad luck; whether the firm would offer any financial compensation and, if so, how much. While they discussed what their answers to these questions would be, one member of the group would take notes to prepare for a final oral report to the whole class. To conclude, all pupils would write their own individual replies to Mr Smith, using their notes and any further sources of help, and explaining the firm's responses to his complaints, stating its general policy in these matters, and giving details of the conclusions it had reached.

In introducing and explaining the task, the teacher emphasised the three distinct components of the task. She first read aloud the description of the hotel and its amenities as they appeared on the worksheet and then asked questions to ensure that pupils had grasped the most important points – did the hotel sound attractive? What were its best features? Was it suitable for a family? She then read aloud Mr Smith's letter and asked questions about the nature of his complaints – what would they pick out as serious complaints? Was there anything in the letter that was not the hotel's fault? These questions were intended to assess and reinforce pupils' understanding of the situation that was to be explored rather than to prime pupils for their work in groups. She then directed the class's attention to the problems they had to solve, going through the questions in the 'task' section of the worksheet (section iii). Chairpersons and note-takers were appointed and a clear deadline was set for the end of the discussion (15 minutes – in fact, more was needed). Work then began in groups.

Discussion was lively and noisy, but pupils were interested and worked well. As you would by now expect, the teacher moved round from group to group, listening in, helping and explaining. Perhaps not surprisingly, pupils found the task difficult. It was not a straightforward discussion, argued from their own points of view. Most of the class seemed to find it easier to identify with Mr Smith and the complaints he was making rather than with the firm of travel agents which had to respond to them. Pupils had, of course, little knowledge or experience of the procedures they ought to follow or the kind of language they ought to adopt. One group had decided to work through Mr Smith's letter systematically, categorising each complaint according to who was responsible for it – the firm, the hotel, or bad luck – and when she saw this, the teacher interrupted the class to point out and recommend the strategy. In the course of the discussions she also gave the class two separate oral cues that time was running out, indicating that they would soon have to reach their conclusions.

The group discussions were then followed by the reporting back phase. The teacher took the class through each of the questions on the worksheet in turn and invited open discussion about the answers rather than calling on each group representative in turn. There were some lively disagreements about the sources of blame and what was the best approach to take in writing the letter of reply. For example, the fact that a smelly, noisy fishmarket was situated near the hotel was regarded by one group as one of the hotel's possible strengths. Previous clients, they argued, may have thought the market was a tourist attraction which provided a source of local colour.

Finally the teacher made the transition to the final phase of the lesson – the writing of the letter of reply. Before the lesson started she had already written on the roller-blackboard the outline of the lay-out of an appropriate business letter, with the firm's and Mr Smith's name and address included, together with the formal opening and conclusion. Pupils were to make use of this lay-out (familiar from previous work) and write their own individual letters. The class was approaching the end of the lesson on a warm afternoon, and pupils were less willing now to settle and begin work than they had been at the beginning. Again, they found this final task difficult. Despite the initial discussion in groups and the more recent plenary discussion with the teacher, some pupils were not sure how to set about writing their replies. Most found it difficult to adopt a suitable persona and find the right register and tone for the letter. Almost certainly if Mr Smith had existed, he would not have been over-impressed by some of the replies he might have received and he would probably would have taken his custom elsewhere in future.

The lesson ended with pupils still engaged in writing and the task had to be completed for homework. The lesson had lasted in all for about 70 minutes. About 10 minutes had been taken for the introduction and explanation of the task, about 25 minutes for the discussion in groups, about 20 minutes for the reporting back, and about 15 minutes for starting work on the writing task.

Case study: 'The Great Escape'

The final example is a more detailed description and discussion of an experienced teacher working with a mixed-ability class of 12-year-old boys and girls. The lessons took place in a rural comprehensive school where pupils are bussed in from a wide geographical area. The unit of work in which the inquiry lesson is set explored the theme of an escape from an imaginary prisoner of war camp during World War Two. The project was spread over a period of four weeks and in the initial introductory lesson the teacher organised the class into groups of four so that pupils could collaborate in 'escape teams' as work progressed. Each lesson lasted for 80 minutes.

Before the inquiry lesson to be examined in some detail took place, two important tasks in the development of the project had already been completed. In the opening lesson the teacher had provided the layout of an imaginary camp which was to be common to all groups, but this information was not presented in a straightforward or predictable way. Pupils were first asked to imagine that they had been captured as prisoners of war somewhere in Germany and had been brought to the camp in question. On arrival they would be required to listen to a formal talk (recorded on an audio-tape made by the teacher) given by the senior British officer in charge of the camp. On this tape, after welcoming them, he explains how the camp is laid out and organised, and he emphasises the rules they would all have to abide by. Most importantly, they would have to accept that it was the duty of all prisoners in the camp to attempt to escape, but to do so without endangering either the lives or the plans of others. He goes on to explain what special dangers are likely to face them, the help that can be provided by the Escape Committee, and the need for absolute secrecy and careful planning.

In the course of this introductory lesson the teacher explained the nature of the immediate listening task and set the context for the project to come in the following way:

Teacher: For the next four weeks when you come to English for this period you are a prisoner in a prisoner of war camp. All right? And your object is to escape. Now the piece of listening that you are going to do today is a lecture or a speech given to you by the senior British officer in your prisoner of war camp. You've just arrived at the camp and he's talking to you for the first time, so he's explaining to you things about the camp, things about the way you work in the camp and what the camp looks like. You're listening to his speech bearing in mind that some time during your imprisonment *you* are going to want to escape, so you're listening for information which will be useful to you in order to plan your escape, and you are going to note down on the piece of paper I have given you all the facts and details that you think would be useful to you as a potential escaped prisoner. Now, I'm going to play the tape once; write as you are going along....

The tape is played and as they listen pupils make notes and drawings about the information that is provided. Afterwards the teacher asks general questions about the most important points in the speech and there is some discussion with the whole class – for example, details about how the buildings are set out, the perimeter fences and the security of the camp. The class is then given a second opportunity to listen to the tape and to check and develop the notes they have made.

The second lesson was more discursive. Working in their groups, pupils first had to establish what their imaginary roles were to be and how they had come to be captured. Then, using their notes from the previous lesson, they were asked to draw an agreed plan of the camp and complete a parallel worksheet provided by the teacher. This worksheet (see appendix F) identified two separate features of the camp – its layout and its organisation – and pupils had to describe in note form the most important features of the camp subsumed under these two headings. When this initial explanation of the task had been completed together with some general questions to remind pupils about important aspects of the speech from the previous lesson, the class spent the rest of this second lesson, working in their groups, completing the maps and information sheets.

The third lesson, which is to be examined in more detail, was problem-solving in its approach. It dealt with the plans the different groups were to make in their attempts to escape from the camp. Again the lesson began with a short directive phase in which the teacher explained what they would have to do and the purpose of a new worksheet she had provided. This worksheet (see appendix F) was arranged under five main headings:

  (i) a brief outline of the escape plan;
 (ii) the equipment and materials needed;
(iii) any assistance required;
 (iv) anticipated problems;
  (v) the reasons they had for thinking the plan would succeed.

She explained the task in the following way:

Teacher: Right, this is where you have to start thinking for yourself. All the information you have got so far has been given to you, now you have got to start thinking of ideas of your own. Remember your object is to escape. In your groups, decide on what you think would be a suitable escape plan, and this first section here (on the worksheet), once you've decided on your plan, is to give a brief outline of that plan, just a brief description of it. There will also be equipment and materials you will need, probably, in order to implement your escape, in order to get it under way. Some of that equipment you might have accessible to you. Some of it you might have to improvise. What does improvise mean? If I say I have to improvise.... Do you have any idea, Paul?... All right, Heather?

Heather: Make do with what you've got.

Teacher: Make do with what you've got...modify what you've got...adapt things in order to get what you want at the end. So you have to write down the equipment and materials you think you'll need for your escape and ideas as to how you might go about getting these things. 'Assistance required' is the next one. What does that mean?

At the end of this phase of the lesson, the teacher emphasises the importance of the final category on the worksheet – 'Reasons for thinking your plan will succeed'. The chosen spokesperson for each group will have to submit the plan they eventually formulate to the camp's Escape Committee to explain and, if necessary, defend it:

Teacher: Now the Escape Committee will not give the go-ahead to every plan. They will assess each plan on its merits... test them, or work out which ones they think are most likely to succeed and it's your job to think of (a) a good plan and (b) to put it across to the Escape Committee so well that they're definitely going to choose yours. All right, are there any problems, anything that's not clear? So your task today is to work out how you're going to escape...

The groups then begin work, discussing what their escape plan is to be, and deciding what they would require in the way of equipment and further assistance. As in previous examples of group work, the teacher moves around the class, listening in to what is being said, asking questions herself, and responding to any problems pupils have encountered. The class works with noisy enthusiasm, but they are clearly involved in the task and enjoy the challenges it presents. The discussions in groups continue for the rest of the lesson and as a result a range of different and contrasting escape plans is produced. Some are predictably derived from books and films, others appear more original but are perhaps unrealistic in their aims. One plan, for instance, involves the digging of a tunnel, another the stealing of guards' uniforms, another a feigned illness and transport out of the camp to a hospital, and a fourth a Christmas party with an attempt to get the guards helplessly drunk with stolen alcohol.

The fourth lesson brought the sequence to a conclusion and involved the spokesperson from each group reporting back to the Escape Committee. At the beginning of this final lesson the teacher again explains the nature and purposes of the exercise they are undertaking:

Teacher: We're going to see the results of all your careful preparation. Each group should now have what they consider to be a foolproof escape plan which they are going to take to the Escape Committee. Now the group is going to come out the front here and the rest of the class will be the committee... when the group has explained their escape plan, then the Escape Committee, which is all you people here, will be able to ask them questions for clarification. You can ask them about bits that you don't think will work, or they haven't thought out properly. You can ask them about possible snags that you see, anything that happens to occur to you. All right?... Fine. Now what group shall we have first?

The rest of the lesson is taken up with the different groups coming out to the front of the class in a random order. The spokesperson explains the nature of their escape plan together with any other essential information and then responds (aided by other members of the group) to any questions asked by the rest of the class. The teacher throughout acts as a potential neutral chairperson, but most of the groups are happy (and competent enough) to chair their own discussions.

The following extract from one of these oral reports gives some of the flavour of what actually happened:

Pupil [spokesperson]: We'll tunnel at night so that the searchlights will be on but nobody will see us and come into the barrack. Then, in the morning at six a.m. we'll cut the wires to the searchlights. With the soil that we've dug from the tunnel we'll put it down our trousers and put bike clips at the bottom of our trousers, and then when we get outside we'll walk about and take off the clips and let the soil out... er [whispering]... We have to dig about ninety feet from the barrack and that should take us into the woods.... We have to be careful that we don't come up in front of the tripwire in case we set it off and get shot and, even if the searchwires are cut, it doesn't mean they won't see us, so we have to be really careful.

Teacher: Right, Laura?

Laura: Where are you going to get the bike clips?

Pupil [spokesperson]: Off a postman [laughter].

Pupil: How are you going to get a postman there?

Pupil: Well, they're bound to deliver some letters there. Shelley?

Shelley: What are you going to dig the tunnel with?

Pupil: A spade from the Escape Committee. Duncan?

Duncan: Em, how are you going to dig such a big tunnel in such a short space of time, and how are you going to dig it from inside your hut?

Pupil: I'm going to move a bunk or bed and it could take two or three nights, but if we just move the bunk bed back again, it ... they won't notice. Laura?

Laura: You're goin' t' look awful fat with all this soil down your trousers [laughter] and then when you walk back with skinny legs...

Pupil: We'll wear baggy trousers. Suzanne?

Suzanne: Where are you going to get all the wood to hold up the roof in the tunnel so that it doesn't fall in?

Pupil: Em [not sure]... the Escape Committee? [Laughter] Shelley?

Shelley: What if the floors are concrete? I bet you couldn't get out then.

Pupil: Doubt if they would. They wouldn't waste concrete on prisoners. It will be bad situations in the camps, so they wouldn't waste concrete on the prisoners...Laura?

Laura: They're bound to see you dropping all that soil out all of a sudden. Where are you intending to drop it all?

Pupil: If you just walk about and let it out bit by bit [laughter]...

Pupil: As soon as you take the clips off, it's all going to be pouring out ...

Pupil: No, but if you just loosen them a wee bit ...

Pupil: That would take ages.

Pupil: There's a lot of time in one day... Duncan?

Duncan: You might look a wee bit weird walking about with bike clips around your ankles. They might ask you where you got them and what you're doing. [Laughter]

Pupil: Well, if we canny get bike clips we'll put our socks on top of our trousers, tuck our trousers into our socks.

Pupil: When you have to climb out the hole that you're digging, your trousers are bound to fall down. [Laughter]

Pupil: No they're not. We'll wear a belt.

Pupil: How are they not going to fall down with all that soil in them? [Soon afterwards the questions end.]

It is a lively session and seems to be much enjoyed by the pupils involved. There is an obvious concern amongst the participants for practical detail and a demand for credibility, even if the discussion lacks a sense of long-term strategy and, understandably, an awareness of the realities of the situation.

To conclude, then, at the core of this unit of work was the central problem which the teacher had posed for pupils to solve – how are you going to plan a successful escape from the imaginary camp we have devised? However, much careful preparatory work had taken place both inside and beyond the classroom before the main problem could be presented to the class. This preparation took the form of the introductory speech by the commanding officer and the information it contained about the layout and organisation of the camp. Further direction and support had also been provided by the worksheets produced by the teacher. And, finally, the solutions that the different groups had devised were tested out in the oral reports and debates that followed with the whole class. Although at key points in the lessons the teacher was authoritative and directive (especially when introducing tasks or managing the transitions between one phase of the lesson and another), on the whole, as the project developed, she had a relatively low amount of control over a lesson's content and pace. She spent much of her time moving about the classroom to communicate with groups or individuals.

There was an emphasis on her responding to pupils rather than retailing information; she attempted to clarify, give support and guidance, and monitor behaviour and progress.

In their turn, although a framework and sense of direction were provided by the teacher, pupils had none the less a considerable measure of control over the content of the lesson and the pace that was adopted. They understood and accepted the rules and conventions of the mode. And they enjoyed a greater degree of verbal interaction with each other (and probably for most pupils with the teacher) than in a traditional directive lesson. They appeared to enjoy participating in the activities that had been devised for them and to work hard.

Finally, as with the directive and discursive modes, a checklist of questions is provided in figure 4.1. This is designed to help you to examine critically and to evaluate your own performance when planning and teaching lessons that adopt an inquiry or problem-solving approach to classroom learning. Again, this can be done in the form of individual self-appraisal, or, perhaps better, in collaboration with another more experienced colleague who can observe and discuss the lesson with you.

Checklist of skills – the inquiry mode

THE INQUIRY MODE OF TEACHING

Planning the lesson
Did the topic or theme chosen for the lesson capture the pupils' interest?
Were there sufficient resource materials available?
Were the resources appropriate to the age and abilities of the pupils in question?
Was there sufficient time for pupils to complete the planned activities?

Implementing the lesson
Were my instructions in introducing the task(s) clear enough?
Was the lesson successfully developed in appropriate phases?
How successful was I in providing help and support while the pupils were working?
Was I able to judge how much progress individuals were making?

Managing the classroom
Did the seating arrangements promote collaboration?
Did the pupils understand and accept the rules and procedures of this mode?
Was I able to monitor individual behaviour during the lesson?
Should I have intervened more to ensure that some pupils continued to work on the task?

Evaluating success
Did pupils work with interest in the course of the lesson?
Did they work with a large measure of independence?
How successful were they in completing the set task(s)?
What did they learn as a result of the lesson?

Figure 4.1

Chapter five

Activity, improvisation, and role play

There is a clear and accepted relationship between English as a school subject and drama. Reading, scripting, and performing in plays have been important parts of the English curriculum for many years. And creating, watching and listening to different kinds of dramatic representation in school halls, classrooms and theatres by means of live performance, audio- and videotape, and film continue to provide an essential part of pupils' educational experiences. Responsibility for drama within a school is often delegated to the English department and many teachers of English are enthusiasts and possibly skilled practitioners in this domain.

Even a comparatively modest agenda for this mode of classroom teaching and learning could be potentially vast and it is important in a book of this nature to be realistic about what can be achieved in a single chapter. Consequently the discussion and illustration that follow will be addressed not to the enthusiast who already possesses considerable confidence and personal skills in this field, but to teachers who wish to extend their repertoire of professional skills and to explore further from a more uncertain and less confident starting point the demands and possibilities of this mode of classroom work. We shall not, therefore, be presenting an analysis of the classroom skills demanded of a specialist drama teacher working with pupils at all levels throughout a school. Rather, we will endeavour to offer an account of how as a teacher of English you can exploit different kinds of 'activity' in a conventional classroom within the context of an extended unit of classroom work. In doing this, we will give special attention to activities which demand from pupils some form of role play and improvisation. And we shall accept the activity mode as merely one further possible approach to the craft of teaching to be placed alongside the other modes already examined.

The characteristics of the activity mode

As the opening chapter made clear, developing pupils' skills in communication is an accepted and essential part of the work of the English curriculum. Obviously, we communicate our thoughts, feelings and experiences to others and represent them to ourselves primarily by means of language – in both speech and writing. But a moment's reflection will show that we also habitually make use of alternative modes of communication and representation. As we read or listen, we can picture or visualise a person or scene, we can experience at second hand sensations like touch, taste and smell. And as we speak, we reinforce the message we wish to communicate and make it more expressive and accessible to our listeners by means of gesture, and facial expression. For example, we may nod and smile and gesticulate with our hands; and our voices rise and fall, quicken and falter in pace as we seek to emphasise or hold our listeners' interest. And similarly, as we listen, we interpret not merely the sounds of the language we hear, but the less obvious cues and signals communicated by the speaker's manner and behaviour. Occasionally, too, words seem to fail us and we are forced to try to communicate by means of movement alone. For instance, most children will understand what a spiral staircase is. But, if asked to explain the meaning of the term, they will (like most people) stare, stammer and stutter, and then a hand will almost involuntarily point an index finger and make a corkscrew movement upwards. The meaning is thereby explained in movement more clearly and economically than by any verbal definition.

Activity and movement are important means of expressing and representing experience and of reinforcing and extending the spoken word. Dramatic work in the classroom, therefore, should involve much more than simply reading aloud a printed dramatic script. It can make use of movement alone, as in simple mime; it can involve the exchanging of roles, requiring children to experience a situation or problem from a different viewpoint or perspective; it can include the creation of a dramatic scene by asking pupils to improvise appropriate dialogue and action without a written text, and by simulating a context and appropriate conditions for a particular sequence of events. And far from taking a class away from the printed word of the drama script and the great works of dramatic literature, all these activities – mime, role play, improvisation, and simulation – are likely eventually to increase pupils' understanding, awareness and enjoyment of traditional dramatic forms and conventions.

From the pupils' point of view, this mode of classroom work appears to be popular and much enjoyed – in fact, like discussion, it seems hardly to be viewed as work at all. It forms an accepted part of the world of childhood play where you are free to indulge your capacity for imagination and fantasy and you can take on and test out a variety of roles from your accumulated life experiences. As with the discursive and inquiry modes, pupils are more actively and positively involved in lessons than in traditional directive teaching. They usually retain a higher measure of control over what happens in the lesson, working co-operatively with their peers and evaluating together what they have managed to achieve. Most especially, as with much oral work, the activity mode creates opportunities for distinction and success for a wide range of individuals. Those pupils who experience difficulties in interpreting the written word and expressing themselves by means of writing, can prove to be outstanding in the dramatic mode. And they can win the esteem and satisfaction that such success brings.

By way of example, let us consider three distinct but related hypothetical lessons, each with a central dramatic or 'activity' focus, but demonstrating a different mode of presentation by the teacher. The first two lessons make use of a dramatic text, 'Hero in the Dust' (Edwards 1972). The scene in question is taken from a short television play specially written for a school audience; the scene is a living room late at night; a mother and father are tensely waiting for the return of their son after he has spent an evening out with his friends. He comes in and they interrogate him about what he has been doing and where he has been. He is evasive and resentful. Finally, the situation becomes clearer and more serious – the police have been to the house, inquiring about him in connection with the theft of a car. His father has to take him to the police station for questioning. The dialogue is informal and natural, and the scene usually makes a recognisable impact on a young audience, presenting characters and a situation with which they can easily and readily identify.

The first example is a lesson which many readers will quickly recognise. It is probably still the most popular form of 'activity' lesson. The classroom is set out conventionally with desks in rows facing the teacher at the front. Pupils are sharing copies of the play and they are all seated behind their desks. The play is being read aloud. The teacher is himself reading the stage directions as a kind of commentator on the action while a small group of pupils read the parts of the different characters involved in the scene. The class is quiet and appears interested; the readers are taking their parts well and reading fluently and expressively. A visitor to the classroom could well identify the lesson as successful and enjoyable. But obviously little in the way of activity is being experienced by the class. The lesson for the pupils is more akin to a dramatic reading of a novel than to the experience of a play. The teacher is the story-teller; the pupils read aloud the words spoken by the different characters.

In the second example, the classroom is still set out conventionally with desks facing the teacher at the front, but the space there in front of the blackboard has been transformed into an acting area. The teacher's table and chair have become furniture in a living room with additional chairs provided by pupils. A small group is performing in front of the rest of the class with their copies of the text in their hands. The girl reading the part of the mother sits in one of the chairs, the boy playing the father anxiously walks up and down. The teacher occasionally reads out and interprets the stage directions, asking the actors to try a particular sequence again to try to interpret more effectively what the playwright requires of them. When the boy playing the part of the son makes his appearance, he enters through the classroom door from the corridor.

Although there is more physical movement in this lesson than in the previous example, the actors not surprisingly experience greater difficulty in reading the text fluently and expressively. They have to try to move and respond like an actor and either frequently lose their place in the script or become stilted and wooden as they concentrate on reading the words on the page. The experience they provide for the audience is more like the first rough read-through of a play with some movement in a rehearsal room than a performance. The rest of the class also have copies of the text and, instead of simply watching and listening to the actors, their eyes move backwards and forwards from their books as they follow the text and watch the actors performing at the front.

In this second example the teacher is obviously attempting to bring the text of the play to some semblance of dramatic life. The play is not being experienced by the class merely as an oral performance as it was in the first lesson. In this respect it is easy to underestimate the difficulties presented to most pupils by a play in its written, published form. In some ways a drama script is not unlike a musical score. Experienced readers can use their prior knowledge gained from earlier visits to the theatre and their understanding of stagecraft and dramatic conventions to interpret a written text in much the same way as an experienced musician can read and interpret a musical score in isolation. The reader needs a stage and actors no more than a musician needs an orchestra or voices. Both reader and musician can re-create ideal performances in their respective imaginations. But if you lack the basic experience and understanding of dramatic forms and conventions (as many children in classrooms do), the words on the page, or the marks on the score, stubbornly refuse to take on any dramatic or musical significance. In this second example, limited though the success of the lesson may be, it can at least be claimed that the readers are standing in front of the class, moving about, and the teacher does intervene to try to improve or interpret the performance in some way. Pupils are being helped to become more aware of the nature of a dramatic performance and the interaction of characters on a stage.

The third and final example is subdivided into two related parts. In the first part the surface features of the classroom are identical to the example that has just been discussed. Most of the pupils are seated at their desks facing the acting space at the front of the room. The teacher is there to interpret or direct, if necessary. The table and chairs are arranged in much the same way and two pupils anxiously await the late homecoming of a teenage son or daughter. In this example, however, no one reads from a text. The development and dialogue of the scene are entirely improvised by the pupils involved. The actors use face and movement naturally and expressively; the dialogue is fluent, confident, and the language rings true. The audience watches intently and with obvious amusement. Many of them see the scene as the re-enactment of a familiar experience. But in addition they are deepening their understanding of how a play works on a stage, how a conflict between characters is portrayed by actors listening and responding to each other. After the scene is over, the class will discuss how effectively the different pupils have assumed their roles in the scene, whether or not the language the actors used and the behaviour they adopted corresponded to their own experience of similar situations, and whether the interchanges between the characters produced a convincing dramatic experience.

The second subdivision of this final example is more complex and more demanding for the teacher. The theme is the same – coming home unusually late from a disco to find your parents waiting up for you, anxious and angry. This time, though, after an initial phase in which the theme of the lesson and the main task are explained to the class by the teacher, pupils are organised to work in groups of four. The roles in the scene to be improvised are the mother and father, an elder brother or sister who has just come in, and the erring younger child. Planning, discussion and some form of rehearsal begin in these groups, with pupils talking about their roles and how the scene is to develop. As with similar discursive or inquiry lessons, the teacher moves about listening to the discussion, answering questions and giving help. There is much noisy enthusiasm and laughter and some confusion as pupils move about. When the time allocated for planning and discussion is used up, the teacher quietens the class and reorganises pupils so that they are seated on chairs and desks, still mostly in their acting groups, facing the acting area at the front.

The groups then come out in random order to perform their improvised scenes. The rest of the class watches. Although every group shares the same theme and framework of events, each scene is individual and distinctive. There are clear differences, for example, in the interpretation of character, in the progress of events, and in the final resolution of the crisis. There are differences too in pupils' abilities to lose their own sense of identity and empathise with the characters they are playing, and in their success in finding appropriate language, movements and facial expressions. One or two children are outstanding, and a few appear awkward and embarrassed. One group in particular seem to work well together as a team; their scene seems to assume a will, an intensity of feeling, and a direction of its own. The children identify with their roles and listen to and react to each other so that the scene appears to develop in a way they had not anticipated when they were planning it. After each presentation the class applauds and discusses how successful the scene was, what was effective about the way it was performed, and how it could be improved. Most of the points are made by members of the class; the teacher chairs the discussion, listens and asks an occasional question.

This final class seems to be more aware of the nature of a dramatic performance than any of the others. They have all participated in planning a scene, in performing it without a written text in front of an audience, and in discussing its perceived strengths and weaknesses. They have watched their peers performing similar scenes and have learned from their successes and failures. When eventually they do move on to work with a printed dramatic text, they will have a wider and deeper understanding of the kinds of experiences the print potentially represents and can convey. They should be able to reconstruct and interpret the experiences that are offered with a greater measure of success than any of the other classes whose lessons have been described. And, equally, if eventually they move on to study film or television drama within a media studies course in school or college, they will have an appropriate foundation of dramatic experience and understanding on which to build.

The skills of activity teaching

In thinking about the professional skills you need to possess when using the activity mode of teaching, it is again helpful to identify three separate stages – planning and preparing the lesson, implementing it in the classroom, and evaluating outcomes and levels of success. As a result of the discussion of lessons in different modes in earlier chapters, it is now becoming clearer that some of these skills are not specific to a particular mode of teaching, but are 'generic' teaching skills equally relevant to different modes of classroom work and organisation. Frequently, whatever the mode adopted in the classroom, an initial teacher-centred phase is followed by the class working in small groups or pairs, and this in turn is often followed by a final plenary phase where results and achievements are discussed and shared by the whole class. Although these generic skills may be manifested in different ways and may vary in importance depending on the teacher's purposes and aims, they remain at the heart of good professional practice. In this section, therefore, these familiar generic skills will be considered in less detail than those areas of expertise which relate particularly or perhaps exclusively to the activity mode itself.

First, then, we consider planning and preparing lessons for an activity approach. If, as we decided earlier, you are not aiming to offer pupils an independent drama course, but you intend to make use of the activity mode as one of several classroom approaches, it follows that you will have to decide how, for example, improvisation or role play can be exploited in your teaching, and how an activity phase can best be integrated into a longer sequence of classroom work. In other words, you will be faced with problems not unlike the difficulties we considered when planning lessons using a discursive or problem-solving approach – for example, what will be an appropriate topic or theme for activity work? What is the best way of using a drama approach to explore the theme? Classroom examples in the sections that follow will provide practical, concrete answers to these questions, but it is also possible to provide some more general answers.

Not surprisingly 'activity' can be exploited in a variety of ways and for different purposes. It can be used to explore important issues derived from pupils' immediate experiences and concerns (as happened in the lesson directed towards the late arrival home from the disco). Or it can be used to investigate topics and themes derived at second hand from different kinds of texts (visual or written). For example, having seen a televised play or read and discussed a short story, pupils can re-explore one of the main issues or situations themselves by means of improvised role play. Or activity can be directed towards an investigation of wider issues or items of topical interest within the community. In this case pupils could improvise and then possibly script a simulated broadcast interview with a well-known public figure visiting the neighbourhood for some purpose. Obvious elements of an activity approach are also visible in classroom examples described and discussed in the previous chapter. One teacher, for instance, required her class to make a simulated telephone call to book a holiday with a travel agent, and in the concluding case study pupils were asked to imagine that they were members of an escape team in a prisoner of war camp and had to explain and justify their plans to the camp's escape committee.

Whatever your starting point, though, as with all lessons, it is usually helpful to provide the class with a central focus of concern, a context for the activity and a clear sense of purpose. For example, in the hypothetical example discussed in the previous section, the family argument which followed the late arrival home of the teenage son or daughter from the disco or party could be set within the context of a project exploring relations between parents and their teenage chidren, and could be a preparation for a piece of personal, expressive writing; alternatively, the improvised scene could simply be a preparation for a reading and discussion of the play itself.

No matter what topic or theme you decide to explore, you will have to take into account one important classroom constraint – the amount of space that is available to you. In most classrooms this is not generous or very flexible. It is possible, of course, to create extra acting space in the classroom by pushing desks to the sides of the room, but this creates considerable noise and confusion at the beginning and end of the phase, and even then the space created will not be large. Alternatively it may be possible to arrange for the class to move to a different room where more space is available and the class can be given more freedom to move about and to create noise without fear of complaint from other teachers. It may be possible to use the school hall for this purpose and some schools are fortunate in having a purpose-built drama studio. If, though, you are confined to your normal classroom, it may be difficult to organise group work in such a way that every team can plan and perform their own scenes. You may have to be content, initially at least, with 'fish-bowl' activities alone, where one group only performs at the front of the class, watched by the remainder of the pupils.

Finally, you will have to decide on whether you will need any resources or props for the scenes and whether these will be provided by you or collected or created by the pupils themselves. Perhaps the most important resources the pupils will bring to any improvised scene is already there within them – their prior knowledge and experience, their feelings, and their language resources. But additional more tangible items can be helpful. For example, it is difficult to represent in mime the making of a telephone call; the use of a discarded hand-set can add a sense of realism and allows actors to concentrate on the actual content of the call and their reactions and responses as they make it, rather than the awkward business of dialling and holding a non-existent instrument which often distracts attention and causes some amusement amongst the audience.

Secondly, we consider the demands made on you of actually putting an activity lesson into practice in the classroom. Probably, the most worrying feature of the activity mode for the beginning or inexperienced teacher is its obvious potential for confusion and disorder. It brings to mind stereotyped images of classroom chaos as pupils rush about in different directions and the noise level reaches deafening proportions. Needless to say, these outcomes do not have to be accepted as an inevitable consequence of your adopting an activity approach, but it is realistic to be anxious and it is prudent to take account of the recommendations that follow. Many will be familiar from earlier chapters, but they bear repetition.

As with any mode of teaching, pupils will almost certainly benefit from clear instructions, from the teacher giving them a clear sense of purpose and direction, and clear targets to aim for. For example, when they begin work at an early stage it is helpful for pupils to have confident answers to the following questions:

What is the topic or theme we are supposed to be exploring?
How much freedom do we have to interpret it in our own way?
What sort of outcome are you (the teacher) expecting?
How long have we got to prepare for the final activity?
How many decisions do we have to take ourselves?

Pupils will also be reassured if they sense that you, the teacher, are confident in using this kind of approach, that you appear to believe that it is important and worthwhile, and that you will value the results they eventually produce.

In the other modes of teaching, even as a beginning or inexperienced teacher, you will already have gained some, perhaps considerable, experience of a particular mode at some point in your educational career in your role as a learner. You will have participated yourself in the kinds of experiences that you are now sharing with your classes. For instance, you will have read widely and should be an enthusiast and expert in this field. You will also have acquired much experience in the business of writing, having produced over the years countless scripts of different kinds, written for different purposes and for different kinds of audience. You will almost certainly have participated in a variety of discussions at different levels of formality and in a variety of contexts. And you will have been required to solve genuine 'real life' problems as a result of your own immediate concerns and experiences as well as possibly being engaged in various kinds of inquiry-based workshops as part of your education.

However, when you approach the activity mode and begin to experiment with role play, improvisation and other drama-based activities, your experience may well be more limited. It may have been acquired passively at second hand; you may have been a reader and watcher of plays only, not an active participator. And this lack of first-hand, active, practical experience may well create a lack of confidence and conviction when you come to try to use the activity mode yourself in a classroom. You may also lack the inside knowledge that the activities involved are indeed valuable and enjoyable, and that they can provide insights and increase understanding. If this is so, it is advisable, first, to proceed cautiously in your classroom and not to take on too many challenges that will overtax your skills, and second, to attempt to increase your practical experience of the mode by working alongside pupils in your classes as a participant, or seeking to gain appropriate experience elsewhere. Certainly, as with the inquiry mode, it is possible initially to focus and limit pupil activity in your classroom so that your own confidence and expertise can grow. In this way, too, your pupils can gradually learn what is expected of them in the way of performance and the rules and routines that characterise the mode.

Pupils' understanding and acceptance of the rules that underpin the activity mode (as in any mode of teaching) are again crucial to your success in the classroom. These rules are related in some measure to working as a co-operative team in groups or pairs, and in some measure also to the dramatic activities themselves. Throughout any lesson, acceptance of the authority of the teacher is essential. As a pupil, whether you are listening to instructions, planning a scene in a group, or performing in a scene, you must accept that the teacher may call for and expect your immediate attention, may intervene and hinder your progress, or stop an activity altogether. You must be prepared to switch your attention away from your immediate concerns in rehearsing or planning a scene and become silent, as the need arises. Similarly, you must accept that the level of noise you and the class as a whole create in the classroom is a crucial feature in being allowed to participate in the mode. And for this reason you must be prepared to control and possibly reduce the amount of noise you create. You must also learn to accept that the amount of physical movement around the room must be kept within reasonable bounds; you are not allowed the freedom to come and go as you like. From the opposite point of view, in your role as teacher, you must be prepared to make these ground-rules clear and explicit at the beginning of any activity work with a class, to remind pupils of your demands as work proceeds, and be prepared to intervene at an early stage to cajole, threaten, and if necessary to terminate activities, when you believe the rules are being ignored or broken.

Again, as with any mode of teaching, your ability to monitor the behaviour and progress of the class is important. If, for instance, the class has been divided into groups to plan and discuss scenes in the way that was described earlier, as teacher you must be able to move from group to group, to help, encourage and advise, but at the same time you must not get so involved with a particular group that you lose track of events elsewhere in the classroom. You must position yourself in such a way that you can continue to see the whole class as they work, and you must remain alert for any signs of potential trouble or difficulties being experienced within the different groups. There may, for instance, be interpersonal clashes within a particular team, or pupils may encounter problems with the presentation of a character or the development of a scene. Children may readily seek your help in resolving a difficulty, but often progress is interrupted and you only become aware of the impasse when it is too late to be of real assistance.

One further dilemma will almost certainly be encountered which will demand your own interpersonal skill, tact and judgement to resolve rather than any specific professional expertise. In considering some of the problems associated with whole-class discussion in an earlier chapter, we drew attention to the quiet, reserved child who finds it difficult to contribute to discussion in this context, but is often happier and more confident working informally in a small group. The activity mode, of course, presents much more serious difficulties for such children. For you (the pupil) are not simply being asked to speak from your seat to an audience of peers, as is the case in a whole-class discussion. Instead, you are perhaps expected to come out to the front of the class, to become the focus of attention, to speak out so that everyone can hear you, and take on the role of another person. It is little comfort to be told (or even to recognise) that this kind of activity will certainly be beneficial to you in the long term, if you are shy and lack self-confidence.

As teacher, you will need to use all your human skills to be sensitive to the problems of such children, to help them to build up their confidence gradually by not putting too many demands on them too quickly, and to ensure that the rest of the class offers them support rather than ridicule. At first, it may be important to make use only of volunteers from the class when beginning activity work, or to ensure that the element of 'performance' is reduced with the whole class being involved simultaneously in an activity either as individuals or in pairs. Certainly, most teachers will accept that the problem of shyness and embarrassment cannot be overcome by forcing children to participate in activities from the outset, and that these problems can increase in their frequency and intensity rather than diminish as pupils move through adolescence and work in mixed groups.

Finally, we consider the nature of evaluation within the activity mode. It can be argued that participation in different kinds of classroom drama activities will bring their own rewards. Generally speaking, it is an approach that is popular with children ('When can we have drama?') and adults already experienced and skilled in the field as amateurs will readily acknowledge not only the enjoyment that the activities can bring, but also the increased understanding of the dramatic medium, the increased self-confidence in personal relations and self-presentation, and the heightened awareness of self. All of these intrinsic qualities and effects seem important and worthwhile, but are difficult to assess and evaluate. For this reason, some teachers will argue that evaluation of a formal kind is inappropriate when using this mode. After all, as I argued in the opening chapter, it is possible to ask children if they have enjoyed an activity, and to be confident from their behaviour that they have, but you are less likely in the short term to observe their increasing sense of confidence and awareness, improved interpersonal relations, or their understanding of the nature of drama. Such benefits will be slow to develop and will not always be clearly manifested.

However, it is possible, I believe, to expect and demand more clear-cut and tangible results. Pupils can be questioned about more outcomes than their enjoyment of an activity. If a scene succeeds, the performers should be congratulated and encouraged. But this is not enough. As teacher, you have a responsibility to try to help pupils to 'unpack' the nature of their successes (or failures) and to help them learn from their experiences as performers or audience. Was success due to excellent planning and team co-operation, for example? Were some pupils particularly effective in identifying with their assumed characters? Was the language used appropriate to the characters portrayed and the circumstances in which they found themselves? Would people in such a context have behaved in that way? Was the climax to the scene effective, under-played or exaggerated? Or, to be perhaps more prosaic, could everyone in the scene be heard? Did everyone stay in character? Was there too much giggling? And was it necessary for a potentially serious subject to be turned into farce or end in simulated violence?

Planning and presenting activity lessons

Although an activity approach, like any mode of teaching, can be applied to any aspect of the English curriculum and used with classes of all ages and levels of achievement, it seems to be particularly successful with younger age groups. As we indicated in the previous section, pupils negotiating the traumatic middle years of adolescence tend to be more awkward, hesitant and self-conscious, and often prove to be reluctant performers in the classroom. When working with these older classes, many teachers find that the activity mode is accepted more readily if pupils have already acquired confidence and experience in drama work in the late primary and early secondary school, if they are at ease in their relationships with their peers and the teacher, and there is a relaxed and supportive climate in the classroom. Sometimes, too, work in this mode progresses more smoothly in single-sex groups.

An activity approach can be used for a variety of purposes in the classroom and in a range of contexts. Like inquiry work, it can be used to explore and reinterpret a literary text in any form (not merely a play script), or to explore a problem or an issue related to a topic or a theme. As in previous chapters, the examples that follow are taken from the classroom work of both experienced and inexperienced teachers, but they are deliberately limited in scope and complexity. As we argued earlier, if you intend to test out this approach in your own classroom, it is sensible to begin with limited ambitions. The mode is best introduced (from both teacher's and pupils' points of view) if the lesson is directed towards clear and controlled goals, if the preparation and planning are focused on a single issue, and if classroom management is kept as uncomplicated as possible.

The first two examples are straightforward 'fish-bowl' activities and show a teacher using a short activity phase within the framework of an extended conventional lesson. The first is part of a unit of work for a first year secondary class which explores the theme 'Emergency' (derived from Seely 1982: Book One, 51–60). The lesson began with the class being organised by the teacher to work in groups in order to discuss their responses to a series of pictures provided by the course text. Each of four pictures shows an individual or a group of young people witnessing some kind of accident or emergency – a crashed lorry with a probably noxious liquid leaking from it and its driver trapped injured inside; two young people clinging to a capsized dinghy in high seas, but waving to onlookers on the shore; a boy hanging over the edge of a cliff trying to grasp another boy who has slipped over and is clinging precariously to a branch; and three children looking down from the gaping masonry of a derelict house at a boy who seems to have fallen and is trapped in the rubble. The caption above the four pictures reads, 'What would you do if you saw one of these incidents?' Each group has been directed to one of these situations only and pupils have tried to find their own answers to this question. Eventually they report back to the whole class in a plenary session.

Inevitably, at various points in their discussions pupils have suggested that they should call one or more of the emergency services and this has led to the teacher asking the class how they would do this. Everyone knows that you have to dial 999, but the activity phase of the lesson that follows is designed to explore in more detail what you must do when you make an emergency call. The teacher calls for a volunteer. You have just witnessed the lorry crashing on a lonely country road; the driver is trapped and probably seriously hurt. The liquid leaking from the lorry is toxic and likely to do serious harm; it may be inflammable. You have run some way to a telephone box to call for help. You arrive breathless and lift up the phone. What do you do next?

There is no lack of willing volunteers. Pupils come out one at a time, first to mime dialling or tapping out the number, and then to give their information and request help. The teacher responds as the receiver of the call. Several children make an attempt. There is discussion after each performance of how you would feel when you made the call and how this would show in your behaviour, your voice and possibly the clarity of the message you are trying to communicate. The teacher leads the questioning and many pupils respond. It is obvious that most of the class have only a hazy idea of the procedures to be followed once they have dialled. And, perhaps not surprisingly, they experience considerable difficulty in trying to give the necessary information clearly and concisely.

This phase of activity and discussion leads on to the conclusion of the lesson. In this final phase the class turns to another page in the course book which provides them with clear information about making an emergency telephone call: how to dial 999 in the dark or in smoke, and what procedures to follow – tell the operator which emergency service you want, give your own exchange and number, wait until the emergency authority answers, and then give them the full address where help is needed and any necessary information. This explanation is then followed by a short script in which a boy making such a call carries out the task in a very confused and unhelpful way. The explanation is read to the class by the teacher and some questions are asked. Then the script is acted out with a pupil reading and performing the part of the boy and the teacher reading the part of the operator. The content of the call and its performance are then briefly considered and both are related to the discussion in the earlier part of the lesson.

The second example is also taken from the classroom of a teacher at an early point in her career working with a mixed-ability class of 12-year-olds in an urban secondary school. The lesson comprises four main phases: in the first the teacher reads a short story aloud to the class; the reading is followed by a second phase in which the teacher questions the class and promotes some discussion about the subject-matter of the story; a swift transition is then made to a discussion of the pupils' own similar related experiences and four short scenes are improvised by different pupils as 'fish-bowl' activities while the rest of the class watches; in the final phase pupils work individually, making notes and preparing to write their own play scripts which will illustrate the theme of the lesson for a possible future classroom performance.

After initially settling and quietening the class, the teacher introduces the story that is to be read – 'The Breadwinner' (Halward 1965). She dwells on the meaning of the title and eventually elicits from pupils an acceptable explanation – 'A person who brings money into the house'. She then reads the story aloud in its entirety, without interruption, allowing the story to make its own dramatic impact. She reads fluently and expressively while the class follows the text quietly and intently. The story is set in a mining community some fifty or more years ago. The focal point of the narrative is a family argument. The breadwinner of the title is a 14-year-old boy who works down the pit. And the

99

argument is about which parent he should give his small weekly wage to
– the violent, brooding father who is unemployed, or the hard-working
mother who needs the money to pay for food and rent. His response to
his father's bullying demands for the money is to pretend that he has lost
the wage packet on the way home from work. As a result he is badly
beaten and sent to his room. Later, when the father goes out, the mother
comforts and consoles her son and it is then that he hands over the
money to her.

The second phase of the lesson is a fairly detailed examination of the
characters and events portrayed in the story (to be examined in detail in
chapter seven). The teacher begins at a general level asking the class
about what the boy had done and why he had acted in this way. If they
had been in his shoes, who would they have given the money to and
why? Some consideration is also given to the setting of the story and its
historical context – why is the boy at work when he is only fourteen
years old? What is the modern equivalent of the boy's wage (ten
shillings and six pence)? She then begins a detailed discussion of the
way in which the two adult characters are presented. The class not
surprisingly finds the mother 'nice', sympathetic and hard-working,
whereas there is little sympathy or support for the father – he is violent
and short-tempered, a layabout, mean, a drunkard. The teacher then
explores with the class the father's possible circumstances; he is almost
certainly a miner himself, but unemployed. Perhaps he has been injured
in a pit accident or has become ill as a result of his work. At the
beginning of the story, before the boy appears, his wife treats him with
contempt and disdain.

Towards the end of this phase of the lesson, the teacher moves away
from the class's understanding of and response to the story and asks
them to consider how they personally would have behaved in the boy's
circumstances:

Teacher: Now a different question. If it had been you, and you were
    coming home, for he's not much older than you are just now, and you
    were frightened of your father... but you loved your mother, and you
    knew what would happen if you gave the money to your father – it
    would be spent on drink – if you gave the money to your mother it
    would save the house and buy food. If you were in that position, how
    would you give the money? How many would give it to the father?...
    So you'd risk getting a beating?... I think 'Yes' say some people...

At this point the discussion and the climate in the classroom appear to
become more relaxed and informal. Until now the teacher has been
confident and very clearly in charge of the lesson, taking the class
through the text authoritatively and leading the questioning herself.
Now the responses become more confused and lively; the teacher seems

more willing to listen and is open to a variety of responses. She makes the transition to the pupils' own immediate experiences within their own families and moves on to the next phase of the lesson:

Teacher: Right. Moving on. This [the story] is about an argument in the home. What do you argue about in your homes? Who argues in your homes?... Don't shout out....

There are numerous, deeply felt responses. The discussion is more difficult to manage and control. Different pupils suggest some of the following causes of domestic strife: time to go to bed; what you watch on television; being annoyed all the time by a small sister or brother; keeping your room tidy; having to help with the washing-up.

In her introduction at the very beginning of the lesson, the teacher had indicated that, if all went well, there would be an opportunity later in the lesson for some drama work. Now, in a brisk and business-like manner she nominates a subject, calls for volunteers, and quickly organises a scene at the front of the classroom. There is limited but adequate space there; the desks in the room already face the front – no reorganisation is necessary. The first topic she selects (perhaps inevitably) is coming home late, long past the deadline prescribed by your parents:

Teacher: Right, can I have a father? A daddy?... Sh.... [Several volunteers] Right, Danny... Mother?... Catherine! You seem in good voice!... Can I have a wee boy... or a wee girl?... I wonder if it's safe to... all right... Ian!... The three of you, out!... Right, we've got the mother and we've got the father.... Come on, Catherine!
Catherine: Oh, no' me!
Teacher: Just come out and shout, as you normally do. Come on. Right. The mother and father are arguing because the son is due in and hasn't come home. So what time do you say it would be? [Various suggestions are called out] Right, make it ten .... Right, so, Ian, if you sit beside this [indicating chair and table], you there... I'll just... [moves another chair] right, you're sitting. One for you, have a seat. You're sitting at the fire, Ian, reading the newspaper. Sh... Right, he's sitting, passing the time. Catherine is the worried mum. She's always looking at the clock and realising that her son isn't in. So they start arguing with each other – what time is he due in? ... Are you ready? Right, who's going to start? Catherine?

The pupils are given little opportunity to be embarrassed. Nor are they given any time to plan and prepare. They are swept along by the teacher's enthusiasm and business-like direction.

The scene is short and a little disappointing. The pupils do not seem to feel completely at ease; their manner is hesitant and they find difficulty in identifying with their characters and in finding appropriate language. The teacher terminates the scene when the boy playing the father decides (to the audience's delight) that the solution to the conflict is for him to spank his son. The teacher decides not to spend more time on this particular scene, but instead moves on rapidly to a sequence of scenes dealing with similar related topics with the roles in each scene being taken by different volunteers. The subjects covered are pocket money, an untidy bedroom, and finally washing the dishes. Each scene seems to improve in the quality of its portrayal of characters, the dialogue that pupils improvise, and the realism of the conflict that is depicted. The following extract gives some of the flavour of the final scene. Two girls are involved, one (tall and belligerent) as the mother, the other (smaller but by no means passive) as her daughter:

Mother: Right, where do you think you're going?
Daughter: Out to the disco.
Mother: Oh no you're not! Get through there and do they dishes – now!
Daughter: How?
Mother: Because you left all that mess there. Get it cleaned up!
Daughter: It was wee Peter.
Mother: Don't blame that on your brother. Go and do they dishes now!
Daughter: No.
Mother: What? Are you answering your mother back? Don't give me cheek or you'll get it!
Daughter: Get what?
Mother: You know what! Now get through there and do they dishes!
Daughter: I did them last night.
Mother: Oh away and you did! That was your little brother Peter who done them last night. Go through and do them now!

At the conclusion of this final scene, the teacher takes some time to calm and quieten the class. Pupils are excited and difficult to manage. Eventually the class settles and the teacher is able to move the lesson on to its final phase. Working individually, pupils are to write down in note form possible examples of family arguments which they can recollect from their own recent experience. This insistence on individual rather than group work has a calming effect on the class and they gradually become quieter as they begin work on the task. The notes they draw up will be a starting point for a topic to be translated into a scripted scene which they will write for a possible future performance or recording in the classroom. For the remainder of the lesson pupils write (with an undercurrent of quiet conversation) while the teacher moves around the room, making sure that progress is being made and answering any questions pupils may have.

In all the lesson has lasted for about 70 minutes – 10 minutes or thereabouts for the reading of the story; about 25 minutes for the ensuing questions and discussion; about 25 minutes for the improvised scenes; and 10 minutes for the concluding note-taking phase.

Case study: 'Village Protest'

The final example is a more detailed description and discussion of a project which involved the creation of an imaginary village community. The project was planned and implemented by the same experienced teacher whose unit of work entitled 'The Great Escape' was described at the end of the previous chapter. On this occasion she is again working with a (different) class of 12-year-old boys and girls of varied abilities and levels of achievement in a rural comprehensive school. Pupils at the school are bussed in from a wide geographical area and come from diverse social backgrounds. All of the children would be familiar with life in small communities and some live in isolated villages or on farms. The tourist trade provides an important source of work for people living in the area.

The project was introduced to the class by means of a traditional directive lesson. The teacher began by asking pupils which villages they came from and discovered that their homes were scattered throughout the school's catchment area. She then asked a series of questions to establish that in any one village you would expect to find a diverse collection of individuals and families and for the inhabitants to be engaged in a range of different jobs – shepherds, farm-workers, lorry-drivers, people working in shops and in the tourist industry, milkmen, and so forth. She also elicited from the class that the community would be likely to comprise three main age-groups – children like themselves, adults (in or out of work or employed at home), and older, retired people.

She then went on to explain the nature of the project they would be working on over the coming weeks and the first main task they were to tackle. They were going to create an imaginary village community and draw a plan of the lay out of the village itself. But their starting point was not to be the buildings or geography of the place. Instead they were to begin with the individuals who would make up the community. Each member of the class would have to create an imaginary character whose role they would adopt in the coming lessons as the work of the project developed:

Teacher: Now the first thing we are going to do today is for you to think of a person, for this particular project, you would like to be. Now, because this class in future is going to represent a village, you are

103

going to be villagers if you like, I would quite like to have a cross-section of people. What do I mean by 'a cross-section of people'?
Pupil: A range of people?
Teacher: Good. A range of people... to cover all these sorts of areas that we have talked about before. And, because other people are going to have to know who else is living in the village, I also want you to give me particular information about your character. Now, I'll tell you what that is in a minute...

The information that pupils are to provide about their imaginary characters will be collated on the departmental microcomputer and will have to be presented in a standardised format. When this has been completed, every member of the class will receive a printed copy of the village's register of inhabitants.

The teacher then goes on to explain how the information must be arranged. She uses the blackboard to reinforce the categories pupils are to use and the order of entry they are to follow. Their characters can be entirely fictitious or they can be based on someone they already know:

Teacher: You are going to imagine that you are a character living in this imaginary village. Now you will have first of all, as we said, a range of different kinds of people, but it will also help if you have in your head a clear idea of the sort of person... Graham? [regaining attention]... Right, you could maybe base it on somebody you know, like your mum or your dad, or somebody else you know.... Or it could be based on a character and then you can change it a little bit just to suit you. But try to have a picture in your mind of this person and try to know how they would behave in particular circumstances. So the name that you are going to write down can be totally imaginary...

The information that she will require about each of the characters is: full name, age, and occupation; marital status (if appropriate) and other members of the family; nature of accommodation – the kind of housing and whether it is owned or rented. This final piece of information will be important in drawing a map of the village and including on it different kinds of housing development.

Once the class had created its register of inhabitants and drawn their maps of the imaginary village, the teacher was able to move on to the next inquiry-based phase of the project. It is proposed, she tells the class, that a developer should establish a new caravan park for tourists on what had always been accepted to be common recreational ground close to the centre of the village. The park will be quite substantial and will include amenities of different kinds – for example, a general purpose shop. How will the characters they have created respond to this proposed development? Will it be welcomed, for example, because it will bring more visitors to the village with accompanying business and jobs? Or will it be opposed because it will further erode the character of the place and the quality of life it offers to its inhabitants?

The teacher organises the class into teams of four or five, taking account of their favourable or negative responses to the proposed development of the caravan park and the point of view likely to be adopted by their assumed characters. Next she informs the class that there is to be a public meeting to be attended by the developer himself – Mr Waterbottom – and a representative of the regional council. What action will they take in preparing for that meeting? What arguments for or against the proposal will they put forward when they all gather to debate whether or not the development should go ahead?

During this phase of the project the groups work busily, noisily, and with enthusiasm. Posters and banners are made, letters of protest and support are written, a petition is organised. A letter to the council is written to book the village hall and a letter of invitation to attend the meeting is prepared to be sent out to all residents. One far-sighted hotelier arranges refreshments to be served after the meeting. And each group is given the responsibility for drafting at least one speech for or against the development, to be delivered at the meeting.

The final phase of the project (and the one most relevant to the present chapter) is an activity-based lesson devoted to the meeting itself. At the start of the lesson the teacher arranges for pupils to push the desks to the sides and back of the classroom. The teacher's table is retained at the front of the room with chairs behind it. The main vacant area of the classroom is laid out with chairs in rows facing the table, as for a public meeting. Many of the pupils have taken their roles within the village community very seriously, wearing token pieces of costume, especially hats. Behind the table on the blackboard and wall the posters and banners produced by the different groups are displayed. However, once she has helped to organise the setting out of the room and the initial procedures for the lesson, the teacher sits unobtrusively at the back of the room as a spectator.

The pupils themselves manage the conduct of the meeting. A boy has already been selected by the class to act as chairman (Mr McSporran) and he is given the co-operation of all the participants. On no occasion does the teacher have to intervene to control the class or call for order. The chairman begins formally by welcoming the audience and explaining the purpose of the meeting. He then calls to the front of the room a pre-arranged selection of witnesses who will present different sides to the argument. Each reads a prepared speech while the rest of the villagers sit and listen. Then the debate is thrown open to everyone and further speeches, questions and answers are improvised. Finally a vote is taken and its outcome declared.

The following extracts from the meeting give you an impression of what actually happened:

Chairman: As you know, the caravan site is going to be built right beside the cottages. As you also know, old Mrs Rosemary Williams lives in one of the cottages, and she is very upset about the idea of an amusement arcade being built outside her house. I would like to ask Mrs Williams up to the stage to tell us exactly how she feels.

[Mrs Williams, wearing hat and shawl and using a walking-stick, moves slowly and painfully to the front.]

Mrs Williams: I have lived in my cottage for forty years and the peace and quiet of my own company with nothing to disturb me, but now you are planning to build a noisy arcade outside my front door. I suppose it will be open till all hours and I need my sleep. I have to take pills now for my ears. The river's noise is bad enough, but dirty, smelly louts and loud record players playing that rowdy music will be the limit. My ears will never stand up to it. I have very sensitive drums. And I suppose an arcade would sell fatty foods and where would the rubbish end up? That's what I want to know. On my front doorstep no doubt. I'd have to crawl over them, and, with my plastic hip, that would be just too bad. I have a job as it is to get out to town now without climbing over papers that are left by the thoughtless and uneducated in our society. And when my time comes, how much will my dear cottage be worth then? Base value, that's the thing. No one's going to want to live in a dirty town filled with punk rockers and tourists....

Chairman: I would like to invite Mr Waterbottom [the developer] up to the stage to see what he has exactly to say about the caravan site.

[Mr Watterbottom, wearing a trilby hat, moves jauntily to the front of the room.]

Mr Waterbottom: Good evening, ladies and gentlemen. My name, as you know, is Mr Waterbottom and this caravan site which I am hoping to build I am sure will not cause any real problems in this village whatsoever. In fact, as far as I can see, there are many advantages. For instance from the business point of view, we will be able to create many jobs for the vast amount of unemployed in this area and the few that will be left over can use the leisure activities at discount prices, as will the rest of the locals. We shall also have a car park which will keep cars from parking by the sides of the roads and many things to keep the children from under your feet, and that's not all. As we shall have many visitors to our site, I am sure many people would like to visit friends who are staying there, and then you can use the many recreational services that we provide together, and at the same time you will get very healthy. Some of you will think of it as losing a place to walk your dogs and play football, but that's not so, as we have agreed that these activities can be done. We are also making an offer to the people who will be living near the new site. If you complain, we shall buy up your property and use it to the benefit of the site. But this will only apply to the residents within half a mile range. Thank you.

Questions are then directed to Mr Waterbottom from members of the audience, first about the problem of litter and then the likely effect of the development on hotel trade. Finally, the debate is opened up to the whole audience:

Chairman: The debate is now open, would you mind putting your hand up, so I can ask you to speak?... Yes?

Villager: Can I pose this question to Mr Waterbottom? If you say this place is going to be as popular, and you have got a car park, that if it is going to be very popular, the car park is sure to get filled up and there's going to... they're going have to park in the roads, and it's going to be a danger to children and animals.

Mr Waterbottom: Well, people are parking on the roads already just now and there isn't much danger to people or animals, so....

Villager: But you say it's going to be popular, so it will be much busier.

Mr Waterbottom: No, not really, because only tourists will be allowed to use our car park, and not all tourists will be staying on our site. So I'm sure there'll be hotel car parks where people are staying in hotels.

Chairman: Any more questions?

Second Villager: I have a question. If some of your residents are violent, what do you propose to do about that?

Mr Waterbottom: Chuck them out of the site, of course.

Second Villager: Yes, but you might just chuck them into one of the hotels.

Mr Waterbottom: Well, if I do that, then it's not my responsibility. It's the hotel's responsibility....

At the conclusion of the debate a vote is taken. Slips of paper are handed out to every member of the audience. They are asked to indicate on it whether they are for or against the development. There is a pause while members of the class write, then the voting slips are collected and brought to the front table to be counted by a small team of tellers. The audience watches and waits in almost complete silence. The atmosphere is very tense. Eventually the chairman announces the result – eight are in favour of the development, eighteen are against. The tension is broken by some cheers, clapping and laughter. Seizing his opportunity, the hotelier stands up and suggests that everyone should reassemble in the next room where refreshments await them.

The organisation of the room and conducting the meeting has taken up the full lesson (about 80 minutes). The management of business by the pupils themselves has been remarkably smooth and efficient. Interest in the project and motivation have been high. The class has worked hard and most individuals seem to have experienced little difficulty in identifying with their assumed characters and the context in which they have been placed. Even though the class in question had not had much experience in working in the inquiry and activity modes up to this point, the teacher has obviously succeeded in establishing a clear and popular framework for the pupils to work in and to an observer of the final lesson alone she appears to play only a deceptively peripheral role in the final proceedings. She herself was pleased with the way the class worked and the understandings they gained in planning the unit together and in performing the final scene. They had gained in self-confidence in performing in public and understood a little better the complexity of the different points of view in a dispute of this kind and the possible action that could be taken to influence events. In some respects, not surprisingly, the pupils betrayed their own lack of experience and understanding, but they had obviously enjoyed the project and were well pleased with themselves and what they had achieved.

In conclusion, as in previous chapters, a checklist of questions is provided in figure 5.1. Again, this is designed to help you to evaluate your own performance, possibly with the help of a colleague, when planning and teaching lessons which adopt some form of activity approach.

Checklist of skills – the activity mode

THE ACTIVITY MODE OF TEACHING

Planning the lesson
Was the topic or theme suited to an activity approach?
Did I plan distinct phases within the lesson to enable pupils to
    prepare, discuss and evaluate their work?
Did I allow sufficient time for these different phases?
Were there adequate resource materials or props?

Implementing the lesson
Was the topic clearly introduced to the class?
Were the purposes of the lesson made clear?
Did I provide adequate help and support for pupils when required?
Should I have participated in any of the activities myself?
Did I provide adequate feedback to pupils about the strengths and
    weaknesses of their work (e.g. by means of discussion)?

Managing the classroom
Was the classroom arranged in such a way as to create adequate
    space for the activities?
How successful was the composition of groups? Should pupils
    have worked in different teams? Should they have been
    selected in a different way?
How successful was I in overcoming any reluctance or
    embarrassment on the part of the pupils?
Did I successfully restrain over-enthusiastic pupils?
Were the activities in the lesson focused and controlled or diffuse
    and disorganised?

Evaluating success
Did the pupils appear to work with interest and enjoyment?
Were all (or most) of the pupils actively involved in the lesson and
    willing to participate?
What was learned by pupils as a result of the activities?
Were there additional personal or social gains for some pupils?

Figure 5.1

Chapter six

Explaining

Although different modes of teaching presuppose different aims and purposes and different kinds of outcome, it is likely, none the less, that no matter which approaches you adopt in the course of a particular lesson, you will find yourself at some point giving or repeating instructions to the whole class, to groups, or to individuals. Almost certainly you will also need to explain the meaning of a term (for example), or an important concept, or how something should be done. And it is likely too that you will ask questions. Again you may direct these to the whole class in a traditional expository lesson or phase, or to groups or individuals when using other approaches.

This and the next chapter, then, aim to help you to communicate more effectively in any classroom so that you can give clearer instructions, explain something more lucidly, and be both more aware of the nature and demands of the questions you ask, and more skilled in the ways you ask them.

The nature of effective explanations

Generally speaking, it is easier to explain how something is done than to explain a concept or an idea. In other words, it is easier to explain (and show) pupils how to set out something like a page of dramatic dialogue when they are writing a scene of their own to be acted, or how to lay out a formal business letter, than it is to explain (say) the nature of figurative language or dramatic irony. Of course, as all experienced teachers will recognise, there is no guarantee that once pupils have been shown how to do something (like set out a script or a business letter), they will be able to do it successfully on subsequent occasions. But at least in the course of a particular lesson it is relatively easy, first, to explain a procedure, and, then, to determine whether or not pupils seem to have understood it by asking relevant questions or setting an appropriate task for them to complete.

The meaning of an idea or a concept, on the other hand, is much more difficult to communicate. An idea is less concrete and tangible than a skill. It is difficult to know with confidence whether or not it has been fully grasped, even though you can again ask questions and set tasks to test pupils' comprehension. Sometimes you feel that no matter how often and how clearly you have explained to a class what, for example, a metaphor is, your efforts have made little apparent impact on pupils' long-term thinking and understanding. You are greeted on later occasions by the customary blank gaze of incomprehension or the amused intellectual scramble to try to recall which particular term the one in question was.

Consider, for example the following short extract from a lesson taught by an experienced teacher. It is set in a secondary school at an early point in the session with a first-year mixed-ability class. The teacher has already explained to the class (earlier in the term) that their course in English will be organised to take account of the four language modes – reading, writing, speaking and listening. At the start of this particular lesson when she is to set the class a listening exercise, the teacher obviously assumes that this prior knowledge will be readily recalled. However, she receives the following responses to her questions:

Teacher: Right, now today we're going to do something a little different to what we've been doing for the last few weeks. Remember a while ago I asked you what were the four things that we covered in English and you were able to tell me... four things... four areas of English work. Who can remember what they were?... If you can't remember all four, who can remember any of them? Helen?

Pupil: Figures of speech?

Teacher: Figures of speech, that's one of the things we do in English, but that is not one of the essential elements of English. Alice?

Pupil: Writing.

Teacher: Writing is number one. Right, that should start you off.... Writing... Neil?

Pupil: Spelling.

Teacher: Spelling is part of writing. It's not one of the major elements.

Pupil: Reading.

Teacher: Reading. Right, so we've got writing, reading... Suzanne, give me another one. Writing, reading... what are you doing just now?

Pupil: Speaking.

Teacher: Speaking. Good. Writing, reading, speaking and... Laura?

Pupil: Working in a group.

Teacher: Working in a group is part of it, but that's not one of the four things.... Writing, reading, speaking... what's the other thing you do?

111

Pupil: Listening?

Teacher: Listening. Four things, good – writing, reading, speaking and listening. These are our four main elements. [She writes the words on the blackboard.] Just write them down to remind yourselves; you don't need to write them down just now. We've done quite a bit of writing over the last few weeks, you've talked to me in the classroom, we've done some reading of poems. Today for this lesson, you're going to concentrate on this [pointing to blackboard] – listening. It's part of a four-week block of lessons. This one will be concentrating on listening. That's why we've got the tape-recorder here...

The teacher's patience is exemplary. She is perhaps surprised and disappointed by the answers she receives. But she refuses simply to tell the class what the four elements are and hasten forward the lesson. Instead she persists with her questioning and teases the answers from different children. From the pupils' point of view, the task is surprisingly difficult. Reading, writing, speaking and listening are obviously all activities that they recognise and are familiar with. The problem is derived from the context in which the words are being used and the teacher's purpose in using them. The teacher is not talking about the actual business of making marks on a page in a specific writing task or getting meaning and enjoyment from print in their class reader. She is operating at a higher level of abstraction. As far as the pupils are concerned, books are tangible, concrete objects. Speaking is something you do without thinking much about it. In contrast the teacher is talking about the 'elements' that underpin and give coherence to an English course in a secondary school – something familiar enough to a teacher, but new territory as far as the pupils are concerned.

The essence of the problems involved in communicating abstract concepts or ideas to children was grasped and illuminated more than a hundred years ago by Tolstoy. The following extracts, for example, are taken from his discussion of the problems involved in teaching peasant children at the school at Yasnaya Polyana (1862):

When explaining any one word, for example, the word 'impression', you either substitute another unintelligible word in place of the one in question, or you give a whole series of words, the connection of which is as unintelligible as the word itself. Nearly always it is not the word that is unintelligible, but the pupil lacks the very conception expressed by the word. The word is nearly always ready when the idea is present....

The pupil must be given an opportunity to acquire new ideas from the general context. When he hears or reads an unintelligible word in an intelligible sentence, and then meets it in another sentence, he dimly begins to grasp a new idea, and he finally will come to feel the need of using the word by accident; once used, the word and the idea become his property....

(Tolstoy, trans. Wiener 1967: 275–8).

As Tolstoy suggests, we are deceiving ourselves if we believe that an idea or concept can be simply passed on or transmitted from teacher to pupils. The notion of metaphor can be explained to a class and examples can be provided to illustrate the term, but, as Tolstoy argued, you may simply replace one unintelligible term with yet another term or phrase which is equally unintelligible (like 'figurative language'). The term must first be set in a meaningful context so that pupils begin to grasp the significance of the word. Next they should be given opportunities over a period of time to encounter the word so that it begins to become more familiar to them. But it is only when children begin to feel the need to use the term themselves to define and communicate their own meanings that the word will become their own 'property'.

It may be helpful initially to think of a skill as a quality that you also acquire gradually but which you can go on improving and refining over a long period of time. A concept, on the other hand, can be thought of as a 'got it' word. It may take you a long time to acquire, but once you have 'got' the idea, it is your 'property' and part of your vocabulary and understanding. It is not possible for you to go on 'improving' it in the same way that you can go on improving a skill. For example, a beginning teacher in a secondary school acknowledged in a recent interview about her approach to the teaching of writing that it was only during her first year in higher education that she finally grasped the nature of a paragraph. Until then she recognised how a paragraph should be set out on the page and what it was intended to denote, but it was only at this late point in her educational career that the term became at last fully comprehended and part of her 'property'. Then she began to organise her writing confidently and intuitively into paragraphs and the concept became part of her acquired store of tacit knowledge.

However, although the distinction that is being offered between skills and concepts is helpful, it is too simplistic. A concept is clearly not just something we 'get'. We also refine and organise the concepts we acquire by recognising obvious and more subtle similarities and distinctions between them. And, as a result, we begin to construct 'webs' or 'networks' of meanings and to create semantic or conceptual 'maps'. We become actively engaged in making connections between different ideas and intuitively relate one idea to another. As our experience and understanding grow, we construct more elaborate cognitive frameworks to help us to store, organise and retrieve the knowledge we are gradually accumulating.

For example, the teacher quoted in the earlier classroom example obviously herself possesses a complex conceptual 'map' which includes the four language modes as part of a rationale for the teaching of English. Within that map, the notion of reading forms an important part. It includes the actual process of decoding print to create meanings, reading different kinds of texts with varying aims and for different purposes, teaching and assessing reading in different ways, and so forth. For her pupils, on the other hand, the terms 'reading', 'writing', and 'speaking' probably exist simply as different activities you engage in at school or at home. Some of the responses she received from pupils indicate that the children concerned are trying to remember terms about the subject labelled 'English' that they have been given in the course of their classroom work. And their answers do make good sense (writing connects with spelling, for instance, and speaking relates to working in a group), but their answers understandably do not demonstrate the same grasp of the principles underlying the course they are following.

Many teachers will have experienced a similar sense of frustration when they introduced theme-based course work to some of their classes. The theme has, they believe, been clearly presented and explained; a variety of tasks have been offered. Eventually when the project has been completed, pupils have to organise their work for final assessment under a variety of headings in loose-leaf folders. Why is it that some pupils seem so confused about which section of the folder a particular piece of work should be placed in? What seems to be crystal-clear to you, the teacher, and has, you think, been lucidly explained – that is, how each individual task relates to an overall theme – is not at all obvious to some children.

An additional source of confusion for both teachers and learners is the complex relationship that exists between 'skills' on the one hand, and 'understanding' on the other. In most situations these two aspects of learning should clearly be interrelated and interdependent. As far as possible, the teaching of skills should not be divorced from the acquisition of understanding. For example, it is clearly possible to teach pupils the procedures for setting out a formal business letter as a sequence of skills to be mastered, but these skills make little sense unless they are accompanied by an understanding of both the nature and purposes of a letter of this type and the kind of language that is appropriate to it. If these understandings are lacking, you are merely teaching pupils to apply a formula or a series of routines the nature and purposes of which are only hazily comprehended. This, of course, was the precise experience of the teacher quoted earlier in the chapter (and many children like her) who failed to grasp the notion of a paragraph while she was still at school.

Similarly, it is possible to teach a class how to spell key words from their vocabulary as a decontextualised 'clean skill'. You can, for instance, provide individualised lists of words and you can organise your teaching in such a way as to ensure that pupils will experience a variety of learning strategies suited to a range of learning styles. And you may well achieve a measure of success. But almost certainly your sense of satisfaction will be short-lived, for you soon realise that some of the problems that children most frequently experience in this field are more complex. For example, confusing the three words *there*, *their*, and *they're* is not merely a problem of inadequate skills (though confusing *their* and *thier* perhaps is). A conceptual confusion is also involved. In order to spell these three words accurately and without reflection, you have certainly to possess skills of visual discrimination and recall, but more importantly, you have to possess an unquestioning grasp of which word denotes which meaning and how it should be used in a particular context.

Given, then, the limitations on what we as teachers can reasonably achieve in the classroom in this field, how can we help our pupils to understand better some of the important concepts and skills that are important or essential in the teaching of English? How can we explain more clearly and perhaps more effectively what something means or how something should be done?

The skills of explaining

Teachers often acknowledge that it seems easier to teach to others something that you have learned yourself only recently, or something you have learned only with difficulty. You are more aware of the knowledge you are trying to communicate, you are more alert to the problems you experienced in mastering it, and you are more likely to be sensitive to the difficulties experienced by others. It is much more demanding and perhaps more frustrating, on the other hand, to explain something to others that you yourself take for granted and are hardly aware of at all, skills or pieces of information that you learned many years ago and have forgotten when, where and how. And it is clearly difficult (perhaps impossible) to teach to others something you do not fully comprehend yourself. Obvious prerequisites, therefore, for successfully explaining something to someone else are: your own confident grasp of the topic; an awareness of some of the difficulties that might be involved in understanding it; and any preliminary work that may be necessary to increase your own comprehension and awareness.

The impediments or barriers to effective communication that teachers seem to recognise most readily, while they are engaged in the actual process of explaining something to a class, are the use of difficult or specialised vocabulary and over-complex grammatical constructions.

Many teachers find that, as their experience grows, a 'warning bell' begins to ring inside their heads as soon as they say something to a class which they recognise will be inappropriate. If this happens, they either immediately gloss what they have said by repeating the information, but in a new and different form, or they ask a pupil to explain what is meant by the word or phrase that has been used. This second strategy, you may remember, was used by the teacher who was explaining how her class was to create a computerised register of inhabitants for their imaginary village project (described in chapter five):

Teacher: Now because this class in future is going to represent a village, you are going to be villagers if you like, I would quite like to have a cross-section of people. [Warning bell?] What do I mean by a cross-section of people?

Pupil: A range of people?

Teacher: Good. A *range* of people [repetition with emphasis] – to cover all these sorts of areas that we have talked about before... [further glossing and reference back to an earlier part of the lesson].

In this next classroom extract an experienced teacher is discussing the poem 'The Companion', which tells of the escape of the small boy and girl from the Nazi air attack in Russia in 1941 (Yevtushenko – discussed in a different context in chapter 3). He asks the class why the girl in the poem, Katya, seems to be contemptuous of the boy, the story-teller, and then appears to realise the word 'contemptuous' is probably an inappropriate or difficult one for the pupils concerned:

Teacher: Yes, she says, 'What's the matter with you?' Um, and why is she so contemptuous of him, Eddy?

Pupil: 'Cos she wants to carry on.

Teacher: Yes, she's quite happy to carry on. Now I said 'contemptuous'. What does that mean?... Anyone attempt to explain when someone is contemptuous of someone else?

Pupil: They want to carry on doing the thing that they were doing before.

Teacher: No, it's much more than that... Sarah?

Pupil: Sort of angry?

Teacher: To a certain extent angry, but still more than that. Yes?

Pupil: To walk furthest, do it better or something?

Teacher: Well, yes, that's true, she's pretty confident that she can go on.... Yes?

Pupil: Determined?

Teacher: (giving up) No, it means that you've got a strong feeling towards the person you're talking to. If she's holding him 'in contempt', she's got a very low opinion of him; she's being fairly sarcastic towards him.... [No adequate explanations are forthcoming from the class and the teacher himself understandably finds it far from easy to improvise a satisfactory explanation of a word like contempt.]

Many inexperienced teachers also express their anxiety about their own very apparent lack of oral fluency when they struggle to explain something to a class, especially when they themselves find the topic either difficult to comprehend or possibly, at the other extreme, obvious or self-evident. You seem to stutter and stumble and find it difficult to maintain concentration and a sense of direction. The only comfort that can be offered in circumstances like these is to confirm that the experience is commonly shared (by experienced as well as beginning teachers) and fluency and control in this field can come only with experience and practice. Hopefully, you should discover that you gradually get better the more you are involved in giving different kinds of explanation. You find that you return to problems and topics that become more familiar, you develop your own preferred routines and strategies, and your self-confidence and fluency grow.

Finally, in this consideration of the skills and personal qualities involved in effective explanation, you should be alert to the possibility that your own preferred cognitive style may hinder rather than help some pupils. If, for example, you are 'by nature' a divergent or lateral thinker, you may unwittingly create problems for a class when you offer improvised explanations, the logic of which seems clear to you but not to others. Most pupils, not surprisingly, welcome what they recognise as a sense of logical continuity in a teacher's explanation. They like to be able to follow clearly the development of what you are saying and to see how the links in the chain interconnect. If you are a divergent or lateral thinker, your explanation may suddenly leap to a new topic or dimension of the problem that only a few pupils in the class are able to follow. No one else is sure where your argument is leading you or why it has taken you there.

There are, of course, additional techniques available to you to help you to reinforce and drive home the message you are trying to communicate in the classroom. The most obvious of these is visual emphasis using the blackboard, overhead projector or other visual aid. Some of the examples quoted in earlier chapters have shown how teachers focus pupils' attention on a particular word or framework of ideas by writing on the blackboard (either before or as they begin to explain) and pointing to a key term while they talk. This was done by the teacher discussing the poem 'Welsh Incident' with the whole class (in chapter two) and by the teacher reminding her class about the four language modes (discussed earlier in this chapter). Similarly you can present a written model or framework of ideas on the blackboard or screen for pupils to use as a guide in their own work. This was done by the teacher who was explaining how pupils were to set out the formal letter to the client who had complained about his unsuccessful holiday (in chapter four). Her oral instructions for the task were reinforced by the framework that had been written on the blackboard before the lesson began.

Repetition is a second important classroom strategy to reinforce and extend meaning. In fact, the story goes that you can always recognise a teacher when you meet strangers on holiday because teachers always tell you everything twice. However, this is not to encourage the simple repetition of important sentences or phrases, monotonously word-for-word, which may divert pupils' attention away from the message you are seeking to convey to your own eccentric behaviour. But you can certainly attempt to communicate important information to a class in more than one way. Redundancy is more important than mere repetition. In other words, you repeat the substance of your message, but in doing so you use different items of vocabulary and different language forms; you try to approach the issue or problem from a variety of directions or perspectives. In this way you give your pupils time to grasp the information you are trying to communicate and you provide them with different opportunities to connect it with their existing experience and understanding.

Using examples and figurative language can also be helpful. When an abstraction like 'courage' or 'contempt' is being discussed, an example offers the learner something concrete to grasp. It helps you to see how an idea works out in practice. For instance, in the following short classroom extract a teacher first tries to tease out of a class of 13-year-olds an explanation of the meaning of the word hypocrisy. Finally, after several unsuccessful attempts have been made, he explains the term himself and gives pupils two practical examples of how people sometimes might practise hypocrisy. He is reading the short story 'First Confession' aloud to the class and stops as he reaches the line, 'God, the hypocrisy of women!' (O'Connor 1953):

Teacher: 'God, the hypocrisy of women!'... What's hypocrisy? What does that mean?... What's a hypocrite?... Scott, have you any idea?
Pupil [Scott]: Saying things like... you... saying things... you... saying that you do something and you don't.
Teacher: Well, it's something like that, only the other way round. What you do is... what?
Pupil: You do something bad and then... sort of smooth the facts over...
Teacher: Not quite, no, but we're getting there. Yes?
Pupil: A person would criticise a person?

Teacher: Yes... For doing what?

Pupil: For, er, doing something good.

Teacher: Well, you're half-way there. It's what a person... it's when a person criticises another person for doing something that they do themselves. They might criticise people for swearing and they go about swearing themselves.... Or they might be saying, 'Isn't it terrible all these people who are stealing' and they steal as well. Okay? So that's what a hypocrite is... So why is Nora a hypocrite in the story?...

Figurative language also helps you to represent difficult abstract ideas in a more tangible, comprehensible form. For example, you will remember how in chapter four the teacher explained to the class that the reading sequencing exercise using the story 'The Werewolf Strikes Again' was *like* a jigsaw puzzle. And although in effect we have little idea how concepts and ideas are organised in any individual's mind, most people find it helpful to think in terms of *networks* or *webs* of meaning, and semantic *maps*. These three metaphors help us to attempt to grasp the complexities of the workings of the mind. We can picture or represent ideas as being linked and interconnected like the intricate patterns of a spider's web, with every construct being unique to the individual who is continually creating and developing it.

Next, an awareness and understanding of your audience are obviously essential if you are to communicate successfully. When you are explaining something to a class, you should never lose sight of the perspective of the pupils themselves. Imaginative empathy – your ability to adopt the viewpoint of your pupils and to recognise or infer what they already know and still need to know – is an important quality that you need to acquire or develop. We are all only too ready to take for granted the knowledge and understanding we already possess ourselves, and, as we indicated earlier, the longer this knowledge has been part of our habitual thinking and store of 'common sense', the easier it is to assume our listeners must share it. However, you should quickly learn that something that is obvious to you, may not be equally obvious to your class. You need to be prepared to make your meaning as explicit and as accessible as possible. It is true, when we read a written text, especially a literary one, we accept the importance of reading 'between and beyond the lines'. We are prepared to infer what we believe the author has implied, to pick up and interpret veiled hints, and to search for a subtext that lies beneath the surface meanings. But in a spoken context the circumstances are different and the immediate demands greater. It is not reasonable to expect the same skills in an audience, especially pupils in a classroom, that you expect in a skilled and sophisticated reader. Children will rightly expect that the information you are seeking to convey by means of the spoken word will be more straightforward and explicit and their skills as listeners will be less severely taxed. Guessing what lies in the head of the teacher is a well-known classroom game, but it is not a satisfying or a productive one.

When you explain something, it can also be helpful if you make different kinds of connecting links to assist pupils' comprehension. You should try to connect a point you are making in class to something else that has been said in a former lesson or to texts the class has already read. You should attempt to create links between the work of the classroom and pupils' own immediate lives in the world beyond school. As they listen to what you say, pupils should be actively engaged in the process of creating their own webs of meaning and in constructing their own semantic maps. But any explicit connecting links you offer will help pupils to relate what they already know and understand to the new information you are now offering them. For this same reason (as we recommended in chapter four, 'Talking and Learning', page 68) pupils should be given the time and the opportunity to reflect on any new information you offer, to talk about it in pairs or groups, to evaluate it, and to apply it to their own lives.

Finally, in any explanation you give, you should be sensitive to the intellectual demands you place on your classes. Do not expect too much of them or burden them with too much information. Conversely, pupils' abilities should not be underestimated nor should children be patronised. It is important for all pupils to be tested out and intellectually 'stretched' and for teachers' expectations of what they can achieve to be high. But if the mismatch between what pupils already know and can do, on the one hand, and what you are attempting to explain to them, on the other, is too great, or the amount of information you are providing excessive, they will understandably lose heart and interest. On the other hand, if the degree of mismatch you offer is too slight, then what you are saying will appear obvious and they will become restless and bored. A successful balance between these two extremes of cognitive discord and harmony is not easily achieved and a measure of dissonance can be both productive and motivating, provided that it is not too great.

Case study: 'New Worlds'

A more detailed case study is provided by a description of an experienced teacher working with a mixed-ability class of 11-year-olds from an urban primary school. Their work in English has included a project exploring the theme 'New Worlds'. This has involved pupils in reading, writing and talking about different visions of the future. They have, for example, read and discussed the short story 'The Fun They

Had' by Isaac Asimov, which presents traditional classroom learning from the viewpoint of children at some point in the future, whose learning is dominated by an individualised approach by means of computer and visual display unit. And they have drawn plans of their own ideal house of the future.

The lesson in question prepares the class for the writing of an imaginative description and narrative derived from chapter three of *The magician's nephew* (Lewis 1955). It comprises three main phases, before the children begin to work on their own stories: an introduction which prepares the class for the theme to be explored, the reading of the extract from the novel and a discussion of it with the whole class, and the explanation of the writing task they are to complete. In the following description and discussion particular attention will be paid to the teacher's explanations which aim to help the class to grasp important aspects of the subject-matter of the extract from the novel and the nature of the writing task they will have to complete. A concise commentary on the classroom transcript is provided in parentheses.

After settling the class, the teacher begins informally, asking the class how many of them have read any of the Narnia books by C.S.Lewis. Several pupils have read widely and know the books well, and more still have seen a recent television version of *The lion, the witch and the wardrobe* (Lewis 1950). This prompts the teacher to talk briefly about some of the different ways in which children from the 'real' world manage in the novels to gain entry into the magic land of Narnia and to talk in particular about the first novel in the series, *The magician's nephew*. What interests him in particular, though, is the idea of the magic rings in the novel which are used as the device to whisk the children away from this world to arrive in strange 'new worlds'. He explains the nature and purposes of the magic rings in the following way:

Teacher: Now I'm not going to spend a lot of time talking about the book and about Narnia. The idea of the magic ring comes from *The magician's nephew* and Uncle Andrew, who is the magician in the story, has in fact got two rings. One has got a red stone it, and the other one has got a green stone in it. [He produces a visual aid – a large gaudy ring with a green stone in it.] Now, don't worry too much. This is not the real magic ring from the story. It's my daughter's... I think it came free with her comic, so it's not quite what I've got in mind. [Laughter] But I've brought it along because it's meant to give you the idea that if you were to put this magic ring on your finger [he holds his hand out to the class and goes through the motions of placing the ring on his finger], suddenly everything goes black and dark, and this room, for example, would disappear.

He has deliberately produced the ring, not as a comic diversion, but as a way of bringing home to the class the real experience of putting a magic ring on your finger and awaiting the consequences. In the next extract he compares the sensations that the magic ring will bring, once it has been put on, to what many members of the class will have experienced in their own dreams:

Teacher: I expect lots of you have had at some time that dream where suddenly you feel that you're falling and falling and falling, through blackness and through space and... have any of you had that dream? [A positive response from the class.] Yes, some of you have. It's quite common to have that kind of dream where suddenly you're falling and you keep on falling, and sometimes you wake up before you actually hit whatever you're going to fall into. [There is obviously considerable repetition and redundancy in the emphasis on falling.] You've had that dream have you, Sharon? Can you explain it to us?... What it feels like? [The teacher is shifting the responsibility for explaining the sensation to the pupils themselves.]

Pupil: Funny. Y'feel as if you're going to scream, but you can't.

Teacher: Good. You feel funny, and feel that you're falling, falling and falling, and you want to scream but you can't. Good. [More repetition and redundancy.]

Pupil: When I had it, I just felt... I just felt all funny, and when I woke up I fell out of bed! [Laughter] I was half way to the floor when I woke up.

Teacher: Kevin?

Pupil: Well, I was just lying in my bed and I just felt as if I was sinking into the mattress, going through it....

Teacher: Good, quite a lot of you know the kind of feeling that I'm talking about. Now just imagine that if this [showing the ring again] was the real magic ring and you were to put it on your finger, suddenly everything here would disappear. You would be surrounded by blackness and you'd feel as if you were falling, falling, falling. But it's not going to be a question of suddenly waking up and finding yourself in your bedroom, on the floor. You come through this blackness and this feeling of falling and find yourself in a new world... a strange world... a different world....

The sequence described acts as a priming phase to the lesson. The teacher has obviously worked hard not only to get the class interested in the extract that he is about to read (and the writing task that will develop from it), but also to connect the experience of the character in the story with their own experiences of dreams and nightmares. The teacher then goes on to read the extract aloud. The reading lasts for about 5 minutes and it describes how Diggory, one of the two main characters in the novel, puts on the magic ring in his uncle's study. For a moment everything becomes 'muddled'. Then he experiences the sensation of a soft green light coming down from above and darkness from below. The sensation is like being in water, rushing upwards, until eventually 'his head suddenly came out into the air and he found himself scrambling ashore, out on to smooth grassy ground at the edge of a pool.' The author then describes in some detail his surroundings. The tall trees are tightly packed and a soft green light penetrates through the leaves. There are dozens of similar pools about him (that lead to different worlds) and everything is silent – 'It was the quietest wood you could possibly imagine.'

In discussing the extract with the class, the teacher begins by comparing their own preliminary discussion about the experience of the sensation of falling in dreams with Diggory's quite different experience as it is related in the story:

Teacher: Now, in talking about putting on the ring, before we started reading this, I got you to think about the dream and falling. Think about the opening of the story I read and tell me what the writer here tells us it was like. He doesn't talk about falling like in a dream. What does he say happens to Diggory? How did Diggory feel?

Pupil: He felt he was in water, or under water.

Teacher: Good. When he comes to, he feels that he's either in water or under water, and what... he looks down... what does he see?

Pupil: Nothing.

Teacher: Well, in a sense you're right... I wouldn't say....

Pupil: He wasn't touching anything.

Teacher: Yes, he's not touching anything. Good. Yes, Kevin?

Pupil: A blackness.

Teacher: Good. So it's blackness down there. That is, in a sense, nothing. Blackness... not touching anything....[Again the teacher picks up and repeats what pupils say.] And as he looks up?

Pupil: Greenness.

Teacher: Greenness. Good. [The teacher now goes on to compare Diggory's experience in the story of rushing upwards through water with the pupils' own experiences of swimming under water.] Now, I expect lots of you have been swimming under water and you know what it's like when you open your eyes and you look up? Maybe it's not blackness underneath, but you can see up through the water, you can see the surface at the top and then you come up out of the water. So there's the blackness below him and there's the surface up above.... Now what's so strange?... If he has been in water, or under water, and he bursts up through the surface? What's so strange about his arrival?

Pupil: He's not wet... or he's not lost his breath.

123

The questions and the responses continue as the teacher recreates the author's description of the scene, emphasising the silence, the eerie green light, and how Diggory feels about the place he has been transported to. He then makes the transition to the writing task the class is to undertake:

Teacher: Now this [the extract he has read] is the beginning of a chapter from a real book telling a story which you'd enjoy reading yourselves. But it's a starting point for us, just a starting point. Because I don't want you to copy the ideas from the book. I want you to start thinking about your own story. So let me put this on the screen....

[He uses the overhead projector to show a transparency which reads as follows: the heading at the top 'New Worlds'; then beneath it – THE MAGIC RING → DARKNESS → THE NEW WORLD; and finally, beneath that, three groups of words in roughly-drawn circles with arrows connecting each of the three groups – (i) How I got there; (ii) What the place was like. What I could see, hear, smell; (iii) How I felt.]

Teacher: So [reading from the screen] 'New Worlds'. It's easy enough to... [pointing to the words beneath the title] to remember you've got the magic ring, this is going to take you into some kind of darkness, the world going 'muddled' or, em, whatever is going to happen to you, and this is going to lead you to your new world. All right? And then, you've got to think of these questions [pointing to the circled groups of words on the screen]. All right? 'How I got there.' 'What the place was like.' 'What I could see, hear...smell,' perhaps. This is one thing we're not told in Diggory's story. We're not told that there's a sort of perfume all the way round, something like that.... And 'How I felt.' So those three areas. [Repeating] How I got there, what the place was like, how I felt. And your journey, there above it on the screen – the magic ring...to darkness...to the new world. Now before we go any further, I want you to copy that down, so that you've got something to remember. All right?

There is a pause while pupils copy into their jotters the framework or structured overview that is provided on the screen. When they have finished, the teacher goes on to explain further what the class will have to attempt to do when they write their stories. He again uses the overhead projector to summarise the points he wants to make. The first items on the screen are the title for the piece ('The Magic Ring') and a suggested opening sentence ('I put on the ring and suddenly everything became muddled'). The remaining points written beneath are the features or qualities he will be looking for in their stories when he comes to read what they have written:

Teacher: I've already said that the title of the story is going to be 'The Magic Ring'... you've got that down already. I've given you a suggested opening sentence there [on the screen] which is similar to the one we read in the story – 'I put on the ring and suddenly everything became muddled.' Now that's an idea to help you start your own story. Now I've put up there too a list of the things that I'm going to be looking for when you write your own story. Can you read what I've put up there? Kevin, you read out the first point that I've put down... what I'm looking for. [He is attempting to vary the stimulus and involve pupils in the explanation.]

Pupil: 'I put on the ring, suddenly...' [The strategy has failed; Kevin has read out the wrong line from the screen.]

Teacher: No, in red, below it... 'What I am looking for.'

Pupil: 'Your own story clearly told'.

Teacher: Good. Why do you think I've underlined 'own'? Your own story.

Pupil: You mean we've not to copy it out of a book.

Teacher: That's right. I don't want you to copy from *The magician's nephew* or some other book. It's your own story. Use your own words. [Repetition] Choose your own words, and [new point] 'Make it as vivid as you can.' Remember when we were talking about Diggory there in the wood? [Connecting link with an earlier part of the lesson.] It was very vividly described, what he could see, what he could hear, what he felt like. You don't have to make a journey through water into a wood like Diggory. You could make your journey through space and find yourself on a sort of moon landscape [example], just surrounded by dust and volcanoes and rocks. It doesn't matter. What's the third point that I've got down there [on the screen]?

Pupil: 'Best handwriting.'

Teacher: Yes, best handwriting. And how long should it be?

Pupil: [Reading] 'At least half a side long.'

Teacher: At least half a side long. If you can write more than that, good. But do your best to write at least half a side. And last, [reading] 'Take care with spelling, punctuation and paragraphs.' But remember [repetition] I want your story to be told as vividly as you can....

The class then settles to start work on the writing of their own stories. This phase of the lesson has lasted for about 40 minutes; about 10 minutes were taken up with the introduction, about 5 for the reading of the extract, roughly a further 15 minutes to discuss the extract, and about 10 minutes to explain the task and prepare the class to begin writing.

The lesson has obviously been carefully planned and thought through. The teacher's explanations are fluent and clear and the language he uses is easily understood by the children involved. The development of events appears clear and logical. In explaining some of the ideas underpinning the lesson and in giving instructions for the writing task, he makes frequent use of repetition and includes much redundant information to drive his message home. Some of his key points are also reinforced by the overhead projector. He uses examples from the children's own lives (their dreams, for instance) and comparisons, like the analogy with swimming underwater and looking up to the surface, to make the content of the lesson more comprehensible. In giving the final instructions for the writing task, he refers back to points made earlier in the lesson and is explicit and clear about the qualities he will be looking for and the criteria he will use in reading and assessing their stories. Intellectually, it is not a difficult or demanding lesson. But there is none the less an element of 'cognitive dissonance' within it for the pupils. The teacher asks them to reflect on familiar experiences in a new way and to go beyond this in bringing these experiences together in the creation of their own imaginative fiction. Perhaps only one important feature of effective explanation is lacking from the lesson and could easily be included – pupils could have been given more opportunity to reflect on how they might approach the topic and exchange ideas before they began to write.

In conclusion, as in previous chapters, a checklist of qualities essential to clear and effective classroom explanations is provided in figure 6.1. As before, the checklist is intended to help you to evaluate, possibly in collaboration with a colleague, your own strengths and weaknesses in this field.

Checklist of skills – explaining

EXPLAINING

Communicating effectively
Was my own understanding of the topic adequate?
Should I have prepared more thoroughly?
Was my choice of language appropriate?
Was I fluent?
Was the logic of my explanations clear to others?
Was I successful in maintaining my own concentration?

Sensitivity to audience
Did I make my meaning explicit?
Did I use explanatory links to make connections with earlier topics or lessons?
Was there an appropriate balance between abstract and concrete thinking?
Did I make too many (or too few) intellectual demands of the class?
Did I create too much or too little cognitive 'dissonance'?
Did I give the class enough time to reflect on and talk round the topic?
Was I successful in holding pupils' interest?

Reinforcing
Did I make adequate (or excessive) use of repetition and redundant information?
Did I quote illustrative examples?
Did I make effective use of comparison and analogy?
Did I make effective use of the blackboard or other audio-visual aids?

Figure 6.1

Chapter seven

Asking questions

When working with a class, teachers constantly ask questions. Sometimes these questions are directed to the whole class in a traditional expository lesson or phase of a lesson, or to groups, pairs or individuals when using a discursive, inquiry, or activity approach. Sometimes teachers ask pupils questions because they are themselves genuinely ignorant about the topic being discussed and wish to know more about it. But it would seem that 'genuine' questions of this kind are not a common feature of classroom life. More often than not teachers appear to ask questions either to find out what pupils do or do not know and understand, or to remind them about work completed in a previous lesson, or perhaps to challenge, stimulate and develop their thinking. Sometimes, too, a well-directed question can act as a device for controlling a difficult member of the class or directing attention to the topic in hand – 'Jennifer, what do you think about this?... Well, if you'd been listening to what was going on, you would be in a better position to answer, wouldn't you?'

This chapter, then, aims to help you to be both more aware of the nature and demands of the questions you ask in the classroom, and to be more skilled in the ways you ask them. It discusses the differences between open and closed questions, the different cognitive demands that different kinds of question will make, and some of the different questioning strategies or techniques that can be used. The chapter ends with a descriptive case study in which the questions a teacher asks and the answers her pupils provide, when they are examining a short story, are analysed and discussed.

Open and closed questions

The distinction between open and closed questions is simple. An open question carries with it no expectations on the part of the questioner concerning the response(s) of the person addressed. If you are asked an open question, you should be permitted to respond with any answer that seems appropriate to you, the responder. A closed question, on the other hand, presupposes a particular kind of response from the person addressed. Your answer is likely to be regarded as clearly right or clearly wrong and often teachers will persist in their questioning until they achieve the response they are seeking. Responding appropriately to a closed question is a skill that successful pupils acquire at an early age in their educational careers. They can recognise intuitively a closed question in class and are willing to 'please the teacher' by providing, perhaps without too much reflection, an appropriate answer.

Consider, for example, the following extract from a lesson with a junior secondary class. The teacher is about to read the story 'Seventeen Oranges' by Bill Naughton (1961) which tells how the narrator stole seventeen oranges from a ship in the docks where he worked as a lad. He is caught trying to smuggle the oranges out of the yard by the policeman on duty at the gates. While he awaits further questioning, locked up in a hut, he decides to eat all the evidence, oranges, peel, and pips. As a priming activity, before he reads the story to the class, the teacher begins in the following way:

Teacher: This afternoon we're going to begin by talking about oranges... funny sort of subject to talk about, isn't it? How many of you *don't* like oranges? [an open question] No one?... You all like oranges?... What do you like about them?... Just have a think... What do you like about them, Kenneth? [open question]... You enjoy pulling the skin off and spitting the pips out... What were you going to say, Hazel?... The juice mmm yes, mmm.... What is it about the juice of an orange which is nice? How would you describe the juice? [a more difficult question to answer but still open]... Well, quickly close your eyes.... Everyone's eyes closed?... Now imagine that you've got an orange there on the desk in front of you. Go on, pick it up... imagine it's really there... can you see its colour? Can you feel its skin?... Now imagine that you've got it peeled... all the peel is off and you've got to the flesh beneath. Now, I want you to take an imaginary piece of orange... lift it up to your mouth now and pop it in. Go through the actions as if you were actually picking it up and putting a piece of orange in your mouth.... Can you taste it? Can you feel the juice trickling down? Yes?... Good... Okay... right, open your eyes.... Now that should have made it easier to remember just what it's like to taste... to eat an orange. Right, now if there was a great big box of oranges there in front of you, how many do you think you could eat just at one sitting?... [Another open question; it will help pupils to grasp the enormity of the task undertaken by the boy in the story – hurriedly eating seventeen oranges and leaving behind no evidence to incriminate him.]

Contrast with this account an anecdote about a beginning teacher who was discussing with a similar junior secondary class the poem 'Mid-term Break' (Heaney 1980). The poem tells how the narrator is called home from boarding-school because of the death of his younger brother who has been killed in a car accident. He goes upstairs to where the small coffin lies and finds snowdrops and candles there 'soothing' the bedside. 'Snowdrops... what do snowdrops make you think of?' asked the teacher. A more open question she could not have asked. 'The end of winter and the coming of spring?' replied a pupil. 'No,' continued the teacher, '... innocence, that's what the snowdrops should make you think of...'. It is easy to laugh at the unfairness of her response, but you may on occasions find yourself also asking questions which you intend should remain firmly closed, but which masquerade as open questions in the eyes of the pupils because of the way you present them.

It is, of course, often useful and important to ask closed questions. Here, for example, is an experienced teacher working with a class of 14-year-olds. She is introducing a lesson that will deal with one important aspect of making a summary – distinguishing important from unimportant details when reading for information. She begins in this way:

Teacher: Now you remember last week I gave you the rules for a summary and we did a little exercise orally? [A rhetorical question – no answer is expected.] You'll find it on page two of the sheet I've given you today. Remember we were finding one word which would be suitable to replace a number of different words.... Now on page three there's another exercise which will help you to do a summary. This one is called 'The Omission of Detail'... John, what does 'omission' mean? [A closed question directed to John. It does not signify that there is only one acceptable answer, but his answer must be relevant and appropriate.]

Pupil: I haven't a clue.

Teacher: [taken aback] Yes you have...

Pupil: [repeating] I haven't a clue.

Teacher: [redirecting the question] What do you think it is, Andrew?... [No response] Rory?

Pupil: To get rid of something. [An acceptable answer]

Teacher: All right. Missing something out... Okay... [still disbelieving] John, are you sure you didn't know that? You omit something, you miss it out?

Pupil [John]: Yes... [not clear!]

Teacher: Dear me... all right, look at the passage at the beginning of the exercise which tells you what you're supposed to be doing....

The teacher is using her first main question partly as a useful device to get the lesson under way by involving and managing a potentially difficult group of pupils, but, just as important, she is testing to discover whether the class understands something fundamental to the task that they are about to undertake. John (and perhaps Andrew also) is either genuinely ignorant of the meaning of the verb 'to omit' or (as perhaps the teacher suspects) he is unwilling, for whatever reasons, to co-operate in the development of this particular lesson.

Levels of difficulty

The teacher in the previous example obviously believed that she was asking the class a straightforward question and appeared to be surprised by the response she received. But obviously some questions are more difficult to answer than others. This remains true even when we exclude from consideration questions that are unreasonably difficult for most pupils to answer because the question presupposes too much prior knowledge and understanding on their part. If the gap between what the pupils already know and understand and the question that is being asked is too great, too much cognitive dissonance is created. But even when we work within the parameters of what we believe it is reasonable to expect pupils to already know and understand, the questions we ask can place different kinds of demands on their ability to think and respond. First, then, it is helpful to think in terms of a hierarchy, or ascending levels, of difficulty.

Consider first, for example, the following short extract taken from the lesson that was described at the conclusion of the previous chapter (chapter six, 'Case study: "New Worlds"', page 120). The teacher has completed his reading of the passage from *The magician's nephew* and progresses to the next phase of the lesson in which he questions the class about their understanding of and response to the narrative and description:

Teacher: Now, in talking about putting on the ring, before we started reading this, I got you to think about the dream and falling. Look back to the opening of this story and tell me what the writer here tells us it was like. He doesn't talk about falling through a dream. What does he say happens to Diggory? How did Diggory feel?

[The teacher has asked two straightforward questions. He requires that the pupils return to the text and discover the appropriate information that is needed to answer the questions. They do not have to think beyond this; they are required to recognise the appropriate information from re-reading the text or recall it from their memory of the reading by the teacher.]

Pupil: He felt that he was in water, or under water.

Teacher: Good. That's one thing. When he came to, he feels that he's either in water or under water, and what... he looks down... what does he see?

[Another 'low order' question. Pupils are again being asked for the recognition or recall of information from the text; in order to answer the question, they do not need to go beyond the processes of literal comprehension.]

Secondly, consider this next extract. It is taken from the second lesson in the unit of work entitled 'The Great Escape' (discussed in chapter four). In the introductory lesson the teacher had played an audio-tape in order to present to the class essential information about the nature of the camp which will be the focus of the project. Now, at the beginning of this second lesson, she wishes to recapitulate on previous work and move the project a stage forward. A worksheet, headed 'Confidential Dossier', has been given out to the class with the following sub-headings printed on it: name of group; name of spokesman; camp layout; camp organisation (see appendix F). She begins with her instructions about how the worksheet is to be completed:

Teacher: Now you'll also all have the notes that you made last week [in connection with the tape-recording]. All right? The dossier, this confidential dossier is your group's information sheet, if you like. The first thing you'll have to decide is the name of your group... what you're going to call yourselves [repetition]... All right, don't talk about it just now, you can discuss it in a minute [control]. Then each of you have to choose a name for yourself... and on the other side of the page each one of you in your group should write a sentence just saying briefly how you were captured... how did you come to be in the prisoner of war camp? [repetition]... Okay? You also have to appoint a spokesman. Then from your notes that you made last week, put down camp layout and camp organisation. What's the difference between layout and organisation? How do you classify your information? What does 'camp layout' mean?... Shelley?

[This is not a straightforward question. It is true the tape recording had presented information about the layout of the camp – that is, its physical features – and its organisation, or the way it was run. But these two terms were not used, nor did the teacher use them in presenting or discussing the task in the lesson. Pupils, therefore, are not being asked simply to recall or recognise information they have already been given. There is, of course, an element of recall in answering the question and they have their notes to remind them. But more importantly, they have to be able to grasp the meanings of the two terms 'layout' and 'organisation' as they are being used by the teacher in this context and apply them to the information they possess.]

Teacher: What does 'camp layout' mean?... Shelley?

Pupil [Shelley]: Where all the buildings were. [No difficulty]

Teacher: Where all the buildings were... from the notes you took last week. Now how about camp organisation? What would you put under that heading, if you've already put all the buildings and the way in which they were set out in this bit?

Pupil: Like trip wires and... [He hasn't grasped the distinction between the two terms.]

Teacher: No, that would come under layout. There was just a couple of things that would come under organisation.

Pupil: Was it.. eh... rules?

Teacher: The rules, right.... The rules that were made [repetition]. Can you remember a rule just to refresh our memories? [A further question to test recalling and applying knowledge. If pupils have successfully grasped the notion of 'organisation' and understand that 'rules' will form part of the camp's organisation, will they be able to recall appropriate examples?]

Pupil: You weren't allowed into the place where the library was after dark.

Teacher: Right. That sort of thing and the fact that? Alex?

Pupil: You were not allowed to wander round the cell blocks after dark.

Teacher: After dark.... Those come under organisation....

Next consider a third extract from the lesson in which the teacher is discussing with a class the poem 'The Companion' (see also chapter three, pages 47–49, and chapter six, pages 116–117). They have already considered how the girl, Katya, is presented in the poem and how the reader's perception of her character changes as the events narrated in the poem develop. The teacher now turns pupils' attention to the storyteller himself – the boy who becomes Katya's companion. They are asked to consider, for example, the age of the boy, which is not made clear in the poem:

Teacher: It's the boy who's watching her and he says that she looks a bit odd, a bit slapdash and she's very miserable, and she's nine years old.... We're never told how old he is. Is it right to say that he must be about the same age as her, do you think? Or is he much older? Or younger?

[This is not a question that demands recognition or recall of information as an answer because the information is not available in the text. However, the first response to the teacher's question surprises him.]

Pupil: The same age, 'cos you said he was a small boy at the start.

Teacher: I did, yes.... But I may have been wrong. What do you think, Sarah?

   [The question has been interpreted by the pupil as a closed question which can be answered by recalling the teacher's own authoritative information. In fact, it is an open question the answer to which can be inferred by reading 'between the lines' of the poem. You have to interpret the situation in the light of your own existing understanding and experience about how human beings seem to behave. Sarah continues.]

Pupil [Sarah]: He might have been just a wee bit younger than her.

Teacher: You think.. yes... a wee bit younger. Now why are you saying that? [Sarah may have simply responded without reflection. The teacher is probing to find out why she has reacted in this way.]

Pupil: Because he was frightened he was sissy, and that... and wee boys tend to do that more than bigger boys. [A comment derived from Sarah's experience of how small boys appear to behave.]

Teacher: [nodding] Uh, huh, you think that smaller boys tend to think about this... yes. Callum, what do you think?

Pupil: I think he's older, because it says, 'I touched the little girl on her elbow'... he wouldn't refer to her as little if he was younger. [A good piece of deduction.]

Teacher: Fine, good.... Sorry, Caroline, what were you going to say?

Pupil: The boy's maybe little for his age.

Teacher: Yes, so he may look little. He may be quite old... he may be ten or eleven, but he may look nine, because he's not all that tall. Yes, that's a good point....

Finally, the most demanding questions of all require pupils to go beyond the immediate topic or text that is being discussed or examined and to come to their own conclusions. They are not being asked simply to recall or apply information they have been given, or make comparisons between new information and existing knowledge. Nor do they need to interpret or infer in the light of their existing experience and understanding. Instead they are required to make judgements or come to conclusions as a result of their own reflections and the evidence available to them (whatever form it takes). These reflections may involve analysing a problem or an issue, making judgements as a result of their own critical evaluation of what they have heard or read, using the knowledge and understanding they already possess, or, in the case of a literary text, explaining why they have enjoyed reading it and appreciating the skills of the artist responsible. Perhaps not surprisingly, these higher-order questions appear to feature much less prominently than other less demanding kinds of question in most classroom lessons. (See, for example, Kerry 1982 and 1984.) Higher order questions demand more from the teacher than the other two levels of difficulty in terms of the effort required to formulate an appropriate question and develop ensuing discussion, and they demand more from the pupils in terms of thinking through their answers and articulating an appropriate response.

For example, at the conclusion of the discussion of 'The Companion', the teacher has traced how the reader's perception of Katya has changed. Initially, through the eyes of the narrator, she is presented as feeble and helpless. She will prove, the narrator assumes, a burden and a liability – 'The child was feeble, I was certain of it. "Boo-hoo," she'd say. "I'm tired," she'd say.' But in effect she turns out to be the stronger of the two, tougher and more resilient, and she also proves to be the leader rather than the led. At the end of the discussion, therefore, the teacher concluded by asking the class whether the relationship depicted between the boy and girl in the poem matched their own experiences of the way boys regarded girls. Were girls in fact in some ways tougher and stronger than boys? And, if he had been working with an older class, he could have gone on to ask more about the expectations that the perception of gender appears still to arouse in us. How does it come about that many people seem to acquire assumptions about the personal qualities which they believe are characteristic of all members of the opposite sex?

Similarly, the short story 'Seventeen Oranges', referred to earlier in this chapter, is an amusing and entertaining tale. But it does also challenge pupils' critical powers. Could the narrator really have consumed all seventeen oranges in their entirety in haste at just one sitting? And perhaps more importantly, can it ever be right to steal from an employer, no matter how common and accepted the crime may be among fellow workers and how trivial and inexpensive the stolen goods?

Questioning strategies

To be able to formulate an appropriate question or series of questions, and to be aware of the difficulties such questions are likely to pose for pupils, are important professional skills. But more still is required of you. Beginning teachers often comment on the difficulties they experience in devising a sequence of questions under pressure in front of a class. But in addition you have to listen carefully to the replies you receive, encourage the pupils who have responded, and try to make use of what has been said to develop the lesson further. When faced by this complexity, it is tempting to prepare the questions you wish to ask in advance and to take notes with you into the classroom. But in practice constant reference to your notes conveys to the class the impression of an interrogator keeping slavishly to a set script. Equally, it is possible for you to prepare your questions in advance so thoroughly and carefully that you resolutely retain this prepared agenda throughout the relevant phase of the lesson, despite the responses you receive from your class. And as a result you fail to integrate their contributions successfully into the development of your lesson.

This section and the one that follows it aim to help you to be aware of the questioning skills and strategies you already possess and use, and to help you to develop them further. In effect we shall be concerned less with how you formulate and ask a sequence of questions in the classroom than with what you do, and how you (and the pupils) respond once a question has been asked. Sometimes, for instance, when you ask a question, you are greeted only by silence. On other occasions the responses you receive can be at best impulsive and perfunctory. There are three possible strategies you can adopt to overcome such problems – directing and redirecting questions to particular individuals; prompting; and probing.

The first approach is self-explanatory. You direct a question to a selected individual and, if this first response proves to be in some way unsatisfactory, you redirect it to a second or third pupil. The timing of the moment you actually name the pupil who is to be asked to respond may be important. It is sometimes argued, for example, that if you name the individual first and ask the question afterwards, the pupil concerned will be alerted but the rest of the class will relax. If, on the other hand, you ask the question first and name the individual to answer it later, everyone in the class should be alert. If, on the other hand, no response of any kind is forthcoming, you can try to overcome the impasse by directing the question to an individual known to be usually helpful and reliable. In other words, it is probably better to say (for example), 'How old is the girl in the story, do you think... John?' rather than, 'John... how old do you think the girl in the story is?'

Prompting, as a questioning strategy, is also easily grasped. When, for instance, you are greeted by prolonged silence after asking a question, it can be tempting to cut short everyone's agony and simply tell the class the answer you wanted or expected. If, on the other hand, you are (rightly) determined to tease an answer from the class, and you find that directing the question to individuals still receives no satisfactory response, you can assist the class by prompting them. That is, you can indirectly help them to recall relevant information, or try to make the question more accessible or comprehensible in some way.

Consider, for example, the following extract from the lesson described earlier, where the teacher is discussing Diggory's journey by means of the magic ring to a 'new world' (chapter six, 'Case Study: "New Worlds"', page 123):

Teacher: Yes, I would have been scared too.... You've put on the ring, and you've come through this strange experience, you're in a strange world, and you don't know where you are. But how does Diggory... the boy in the story feel?... How about Grant? Let's have an answer from you. How do you think Diggory seems to feel?
[The question has been directed to Grant. It is not clear why Grant has been selected. It may be a deliberate attempt to draw a quieter pupil into the discussion or it may be a control device to regain Grant's wandering attention.]

Pupil [Grant]: He felt that he belonged there.

Teacher: Yes, good, he's not frightened at all. He feels he belongs there. He feels as if he's been there a long, long time. So he's not feeling nervous or anxious at all.... And what's the strange thing he says about this place? [Not a clear question. Are the pupils forced to try to guess what is in the teacher's head?]... He says it's *like* what? [A prompt – he is looking for a simile of some kind.] Yes?

Pupil: The trees are growing around him. He feels that the trees are growing and drinking the water.

Teacher: Good, that's one thing. [But obviously not the answer the teacher wants.] Yes, he feels that he can almost feel the trees drinking up the water and he says the place is er... I'm sorry what were you going to say?

Pupil: I was going to say that he felt like he'd been there for ever.

Teacher: Good, yes, he's only been there for minutes, but feels as if he's been there for ever. [He has still not received the answer he wanted.] And what's the strange comparison he uses...? [An additional prompt – the simile is 'strange'.] He says it's rich... rich like what? [A final prompt – he is beginning to quote directly from the text.]

Pupil: Like a plum cake.

Teacher: Like a plum cake.... Well, fine....

The final strategy in this section is probing. As the term suggests, this entails encouraging a pupil, who has responded to a question with an answer that is abrupt or limited in depth or scope, to be clearer or more explicit, or to develop the answer in greater detail. You want pupils to say more, to 'unpack' what they take for granted, or to explain or justify what they have said. The following short extract from the discussion of 'The Companion' shows the strategy in use:

Teacher: Why does [the storyteller] decide to look after [Katya]?... [Hands go up.] Let's have someone else... Hazel, why do you think he decides to look after her? [The question has been directed to a particular pupil.] Remember, we're seeing the story through the boy's eyes... it's the boy who's saying this [a prompt]. Why does he feel that he's got to do something.... Well, Sarah, you? [No response from Hazel; the question is redirected to Sarah.]

Pupil [Sarah]: Well, it says in the poem that he thought that in some sense she was human.

[This answer is almost a direct quotation from the poem. It does not show for sure that she has fully understood the storyteller's motives. The teacher therefore probes further.]

Teacher: Yes, so what sort of impression does that give you about how he thinks about small girls?

Pupil [Sarah]: Well, he thinks they're sissy and they're not really human.

Teacher: Yes, he thinks they're sissy and not really human.... So he decides that he's got to do something about this silly girl.... [He is satisfied with her answer, repeats it, and then develops it further.]

Responding

Asking a question presupposes some kind of answer, and an answer in its turn anticipates some kind of response from the questioner. When you are dealing with pupils' answers to your questions in the classroom, it is easy to overlook the importance of the way you yourself respond. As we indicated earlier, the management of a questioning phase in a classroom is complex and demanding. If you are working with the whole class, you have to monitor the behaviour and responses of the pupils continuously throughout the questioning phase, and you have to be prepared to take appropriate action if you feel concentration or interest is flagging. And at the same time you have to try to formulate your questions and maintain the momentum of the lesson. It is understandable, therefore, if you sometimes seem to ignore or undervalue some of the answers pupils offer. This can be especially true if these answers do not conform to your expectations or to the plans you have made (or are still constructing) for the development of your lesson. In fact some beginning teachers seem to be so intent on formulating and delivering the questions they want to ask that the contribution made to the process by pupils' answers is brushed quickly aside to make room for the next question.

In this section, therefore, we consider some of the ways in which your responses, as teacher, can encourage your pupils in a questioning phase of a lesson and can facilitate their learning. And we also consider the pupils' point of view in order to explore further how they can be helped to respond to a teacher's questions more successfully and effectively.

When you respond to pupils' answers to your questions, the most obvious quality that is demanded of you is that you show that you are listening to them and are interested in what they have to say. Clearly you will communicate this interest by what you say by way of reply, but also by your manner and your behaviour. You will almost certainly look directly at the child who is answering, you may perhaps also nod and smile, and you may give some verbal encouragement for the pupil to continue. Above all, when pupils have said what they want to say, you should (generally speaking) encourage and 'reward' them for their contribution. It is true, sometimes a pupil's answer can be deliberately unhelpful or provocative, and it is not unknown for children to attempt to side-track a teacher so that the lesson veers off in a new and perhaps less demanding direction. Under these circumstances, clearly, it would be inappropriate to offer any encouragement or reward to the pupils concerned. In any case, their behaviour may well already have gained them the attention they are seeking.

In most circumstances, though, pupils do deserve some form of encouragement and reward when they respond to your questions. As I indicated in earlier chapters, for some children the effort involved in speaking up in front of the whole class, making themselves heard and overcoming any natural shyness, is considerable. In fact, for a beginning teacher, any answer that breaks what may appear to be an eternity of silence seems welcome. For this reason you may find that you develop routine responses and habits of speech which you tend to over-use. Pupils learn that it is not the word or phrase itself that carries significance, but the way it is spoken – the intonation, emphasis, and facial expression. For example, when I came to analyse my own class-room behaviour after video-recording lessons, I discovered that in responding to pupils in a questioning phase I used the word 'good' in at least three distinct ways – (i) to indicate that I was pleased with the answer; (ii) to show that I was pleased the pupil had replied, but that I was less pleased with the content of the answer; and (iii) to communicate that I was relieved someone had said something, but that really the reply had no relevance to the question I had asked. From the pupil's point of view, though, encouragement is important, even if your answer turns out to be regarded as inappropriate (or simply wrong); your reward can be taken from what the teacher says to you or from how he or she behaves. ('Rewards' in this context are not likely to be tangible or concrete in form!) And, finally, it can be important, when you receive a reply from a pupil that surprises you because it is both unusual and unanticipated, that you share this surprise and interest with the class. ('Well, yes, I'd never really thought about it like that.... Good, let's think about that for a minute....')

Your responses to pupils' answers can also assist in developing further their own understanding. At one very basic level, especially in a questioning phase with the whole class, it is important to ensure that everyone can hear what is being said. Pupils will not normally experience any problems in hearing you, the teacher, but it is often difficult for everyone to pick up what individual children say when they reply. In these circumstances it may be important for you to relay back to the rest of the class what has been said. More importantly, though, you can take up one particular aspect of what a child has said, either to highlight an important feature in the reply, or to extend the answer by means of your own comments, or to relate it to existing knowledge or the subject-matter of earlier lessons. In these ways you are developing further a pupil's intended meaning, or making it clearer and more explicit, or setting the answer in a wider, more ambitious context. In such cases, your aim is not simply to respond, but to explain too. And, as in the case of deliberate classroom explanations (discussed in the previous chapter), you are helping pupils to construct their own conceptual or semantic maps, and to make appropriate connections between what is being discussed in class and recently acquired or existing knowledge and understanding.

Consider, for example, the following extract from the lesson which introduced the village project discussed earlier (chapter five, 'Village Protest,' page 103). Having got the lesson under way by asking pupils which villages they themselves came from, the teacher then went on to explore the different kinds of people that make up any community:

Teacher: Right, so we have got another lot of people, shopkeepers, haven't we? And in this particular area we have got another whole lot of people connected with another industry... Claire, can you concentrate? [Question to establish control] Another industry that is connected with this area. We have talked about agriculture, what is the other big industry connected with this area? [The teacher is not encouraging pupils simply to talk about different kinds of people. She is organising the discussion at a higher level of abstraction – not 'farms and farmers' but 'agriculture'.]

Pupil: Tourists.

Teacher: Tourism. ['Tourism' not 'tourists'.] So what else have we got people in villages doing? [Request for examples] Go on, Gemma. [Encouragement]

Pupil [Gemma]: Hotels, guest houses...

Teacher: Hotels, guest houses, restaurants, bed and breakfast places [Gemma's answer has been developed further]. Scott?

Pupil [Scott]: Milkmen. [Perhaps an unexpected reply.]

Teacher: Yes, all villages probably have somebody that delivers milk. [Scott has not been discouraged, but the teacher's response is non-committal.] Robert, what were you going to say?

Pupil [Robert]: Paper-boys.

Teacher: Paper-boys?... Yes. [Again, Robert has not been discouraged, but his reply is similar to Scott's. The lesson does not seem to be developing in the direction the teacher intended.] Now, what Robert's brought in there is a different category of people altogether. [She has decided to make use of Robert's answer to push the discussion back to a higher level of abstraction – 'categories of people'; a reward to Robert.] Because all the people you have given me so far tend to be people that have jobs c⁴ work and they are therefore all... Margaret? [The teacher has developed further what pupils have said and she has reorganised their points, highlighting one particular aspect.]

Pupil [Margaret]: [Reply not clear]

Teacher: Adults, right. [Relaying Margaret's answer to the rest of the class and reinforcing it] And Robert brought in another set of people there and talked about what? [Another reward to Robert]... With the paper-boy... Fiona?

Pupil [Fiona]: Children.

Teacher: Children, right. [Encouragement] So we have got adults, we have got children. The adults do a range of jobs. Do all adults do jobs?

Pupil: No.

Teacher: So what... what sort of adults don't do jobs?

Pupil: The unemployed. [Perhaps not the answer she expected.]

Teacher: People that are unemployed. That's one section of adults that don't do jobs. [The pupil has not been discouraged; a new category has been established.] Sandy?

Pupil [Sandy]: OAPs... people who have retired.

Teacher: People who have retired from jobs, who are too old now or have given up their jobs and are enjoying their retirement.... So we have got people who *do* work, people who *don't* do work for one reason or another, we have got people who are at school like yourselves.... [She has offered a summary of what has been said.] Yes?

Pupil: Mums.

Teacher: Yes, who do a job of work, but they don't go *out* to work. People who stay at home and look after you, provide you with your meals and that sort of thing.... Probably a very hard job. [The teacher has picked up the pupil's reply and developed it in order to make a further point about the role of women in the home.] So we have got all those sorts of people....

Finally in this section, it is important to view the process of asking and responding to questions in the classroom from the pupil's point of view as well as the teacher's. In your role as pupil, you too (ideally) are listening, trying to make sense of the questions that are being asked, trying to follow the logic of the development of the lesson, and attempting to formulate replies that will be judged by the teacher to be relevant and appropriate. The 'climate' that the teacher will have established in the classroom and your knowledge of the teacher's likely response, are both factors which are likely to influence you when you decide whether or not you are going to volunteer a reply. You will be aware, for instance, of the kinds of reactions pupils have received in the past when they have attempted to make similar contributions and this understanding will help you to decide whether you in your turn will respond or remain silent. Even if a question is directed to you personally, a reply is not always essential. A successful strategy in such circumstances (much used by some pupils) is to keep your head well down and remain silent in the confident expectation that the teacher will lose patience and redirect the question to someone else. You may intuitively realise, too, that some teachers tend to direct questions to pupils they know will respond and will have something helpful and sensible to say.

Assuming, though, that the classroom climate is positive and encouraging, and that you, the pupil, are prepared to participate orally in the lesson, how do you successfully interpret the nature and purpose of a teacher's question? For example, you will probably take open and closed questions at their face value and will be willing to respond in a way that seems to you to be appropriate. But it is now rightly argued that pupils will need more help from the teacher in identifying the nature of different kinds of question and, more importantly, in understanding what will count as a relevant and appropriate reply (Leahy 1988). In much the same way that teachers need to be aware of the different levels of difficulty that their own questions pose, pupils in their turn need to understand that different sources of knowledge or information are available to them to draw on when they make their replies.

A simple framework has been proposed which can be communicated to pupils to alert them to these different sources of knowledge that they can exploit (see, for example, Pearson and Johnson 1978: 157). Once the framework has been grasped, pupils will have to decide how it can be best applied. They will have to determine which of the sources available to them is the most appropriate when they come to answer a particular question. The three sources are presented in the following way:

(i) the answer is 'right there' – the necessary material has been made explicit and is immediately available in the lesson or in a text being studied; the question demands only that you recall or recognise the relevant information;

(ii) 'think and search' – the information is not clearly available or explicit; in order to answer the question you have to think back and possibly bring together different pieces of information from different sources;

(iii) 'on my own' or 'in my head' – here you have to go beyond any information provided in the lesson; you have to connect it with the knowledge and understanding you have already accumulated both within and beyond school.

Clearly, these three different kinds of resource that are available to pupils are not unlike the three levels of difficulty that were proposed earlier in the chapter and presented from the teacher's rather than the pupil's perspective – low order, middle order, and high order questions. Both frameworks reflect an increasing level of difficulty, making gradually greater demands on both questioner and responder alike. As the gradient of difficulty increases, so you are asked to go beyond the recognition and recall of specific explicit information, to the reorganisation, application and interpretation of given information and the making of inferences, until you reach the summit where you are required to evaluate information independently or appreciate what has been achieved.

Case study: 'The Breadwinner'

The final section in this chapter presents a detailed examination and discussion of part of a lesson that will already be familiar to you from chapter five. In the first phase of this extended lesson the teacher concerned read the short story 'The Breadwinner' (Halward 1965) to her mixed-ability class of 12-year-olds in an urban comprehensive school. She then went on to discuss the story in some detail before getting the class to improvise their own scenes based on the theme 'Family Quarrel'. You will remember that the story, set about fifty years ago, describes how a 14-year-old boy returns from work with his first wage packet – an important source of income for the family – and is involved in a violent family quarrel. Both his father and his mother demand the money, but rather than hand it over to his drunken father, the boy pretends that he has lost it on his journey home. As a result he is beaten by his father. Later, when he is alone with his mother and is being comforted by her, he hands the money over to pay for the rent and food.

We are to look closely at the part of the lesson in which the teacher is questioning the class about the way the mother is presented in the story and their own responses to her. It is a directive phase in which the teacher works with the whole class. Pupils have copies of the text to which they can refer. As before, a commentary is provided in parentheses:

Teacher: What can you tell me about the mother? Have a look at what it says. Try not to give me just the words used in the story... tell me what kind of person she is. [A middle order question – the answer is not provided in the text; pupils have to reflect on how the mother is presented in different incidents and come to their own conclusion.]

Pupil: She's a nice lady. She's not like the father who's nasty. [An acceptable but vague response.]

Teacher: Right, she's nice. [The pupil has been encouraged.] What example do we have of her being nice? [Pupils are being asked to apply the conclusion that one of them has rcached to the text; the teacher demands more in the way of justification and explicit detail.] Sandy? [The question is directed to a different pupil.]

Pupil [Sandy]: She went to the boy when he was going to be belted.

Teacher: Right [encouragement]. She came up to the wee boy, right after the man had gone, and cuddled him.

Pupil: She stuck up for him.

Teacher: She stuck up for him. Where? When?... When did she stick up for him? [Again she demands more detail.]

Pupil: When he was going to get the belt.

Teacher: Just the minute before he was going to get belted, she rushed forward and tried to stop the man, but of course he was too strong for her. [She has taken up the pupil's answer and developed it further.] More about the mother being a nice lady. [She is probing further.]

Pupil: Once the boy got belted, she said he wanted food.

Teacher: Mmm, right [encouragement]. The mother realised that the boy had actually been out working all day and he deserved some food. In the end who got the food? [Low order question – the information is clearly available in the story.]

Pupil: The father.

Teacher: The father.... And what food did he have? [Another low order question; we are told in the story.]

Pupil: Two slices of bread and a cup of tea.

Teacher: So that would tie in with the title 'The Breadwinner'. In fact, here he's actually eating the bread. [A connecting link has been made with the opcning of the lesson, before the story had been read, when the teacher had asked the class what they thought the title meant.] More about the woman, though. [She is probing further.]

Pupil: She was worried about the family, and using the money for the rent.

Teacher: She was more concerned about the family and wanting to put the money for rent. [She has repeated the answer and relayed it clearly to the whole class.]

Pupil: She was very tired.

Teacher: Right [accepting the answer], where's the evidence that she's tired? [Probing further]... Colin? [The question is directed to a specific individual.]

Pupil [Colin]: In the second paragraph.

Teacher: Right [accepting the answer again, but wanting to probe further], whereabouts?... Read the bit out.

Pupil [Colin – reading]: 'She was a little woman with a pinched face and a spare body....'

Teacher: Right, if we go through the description of the woman. 'Pinched face'... what does that mean? She had a pinched face.... [Not an easy question. The word 'pinched' is almost certainly used in a different way by pupils. They have to reflect on what it means in this particular context.] Come on, some of you are half asleep! Who can answer?

Pupil: A sad face?

Teacher: A sad face? A wee bit more than just a sad face. [The answer has not been accepted, but the pupil has nct been discouraged as a result.]

Pupil: Thin?

Teacher: Right, very thin. Almost as if she had sucked her cheeks in. You could almost see the bones in her face. [The teacher has accepted and developed the answer, helping the class to visualise the mother's physical appearance more clearly.] 'A spare body'.... What does that mean?... She had a spare body? [Another difficult question which requires interpretation, matching the use of the words in this particular context with pupils' own existing understanding of how the words are normally used. It causes some confusion.]

Pupil: Stout?

Teacher [surprised]: She was stout? How do you get from a spare body that she was stout? [An open and perhaps a 'genuine' question; the teacher does not follow the pupil's thinking.] What makes you think she's fat?

Pupil: She's got a broad face and she just looks as if she's fat. [Not an answer that is likely to help the teacher.]

Teacher: She looks as though she's fat? [She is still uncertain.] Can anybody tell me what Bob is thinking of 'spare' as meaning? [An appeal to the whole class.]

Pupil: She's so fat it looks as if she's got two bodies.

Teacher [beginning to understand]: Right, she's so big she looks as if she's got two bodies... in other words, a spare tyre? Yes? [Nodded and murmured assent from some members of the class. The teacher continues forcefully but with good humour.] Well... you're wrong! The spare body means...? [She is not yet willing to give up and probes further.]

Pupil: That she works?

Teacher: She works.... Well, that means what? [probing]

Pupil: She's thin.

Teacher: She's thin... Yes! If you think about it, how *must* she be thin? Why would it be difficult for her to be fat? [Another demanding middle order question. Pupils are being asked to take information from the whole story and make deductions from it about why the woman is described in this way. The success of their deductions will depend on their own understanding of the effects of hard work and poverty and their ability to connect this knowledge with the discussion about the story.]

Pupil: She doesn't get enough food.

Teacher: Right, she doesn't get much to eat... and? [Probing further] You said it before, David.... You've forgotten already? [She has directed the question to another individual and is making a connection with something he has said a little earlier in the lesson.]

Pupil [David]: She works.

Teacher: Right, she's always on the go. She dresses [quoting] 'in a blue blouse and skirt, the front of the skirt covered with a starched white apron.' If I tell you that those four words.... 'a starched white apron'.... tell us so much about the woman. Can you tell me what it is? [Another middle order question demanding inference. Pupils have to use their own existing understanding to infer what the quotation from the text tells the reader about the mother's character.] If you're playing detectives, remember whenever you look at a story you've got to pick up clues, and they tell you more about the people and the things in the story. [She has highlighted or emphasised for the class an important reading strategy.] What does the fact that she wears a starched white apron tell us about the woman?

Pupil: She's clean? [The pupil has responded only to the literal information provided in the quotation; he has not inferred.]

Teacher: She's always clean, that's one part. [The addition of the word 'always' is a significant development of what the pupil said; it is itself an inference.] Can you tell me more? [Probing for more information.]

Pupil: Her clothes aren't clean... because she hasn't got a washing machine.

Teacher [surprised]: Her clothes *aren't* clean? [The pupil has made an inference, but an incorrect one – she has assumed that if you have not got a washing machine, it must be impossible to be clean.] But it says 'starched white apron', which means? [A prompt.]

Pupil: That it *is* clean...

Teacher: But the second point's important; she doesn't have a washing machine. [She takes up the pupil's earlier answer and makes use of it to develop the discussion in a different way.] When do you think the story takes place? [A middle order question; the reader is not given the answer in the text. Again pupils have to infer, matching their existing historical knowledge to any clues they can pick up from the text. It is a 'think and search' question.]

Pupil: All the time. [A flip answer or a very profound one?]

Pupil: The thirties' depression.

Teacher: The thirties' depression.... Why? [Probing]

Pupil: Because the children go out to work.

Teacher: The children were working. He's fourteen, so he's not at school in those days.

Pupil: They owed money – ten shillings and sixpence.

Teacher: Good. They owed money. Ten shillings and sixpence.... [There is a short digression while pupils work out the current value of the sum.] Right! So, it takes place in the thirties, she doesn't have a washing machine.... So we've got a wee bit away from the point [regaining her sense of direction]... why does the fact that's she's wearing a starched white apron and she doesn't have a washing machine tell us she's a very good woman? [An 'on my own' question? There is no information in the text to help pupils. They have to connect the starched white apron with the notion of 'goodness' and come up with an appropriate answer.]

Pupil: She goes to the laundry or something to do all her washing.

Teacher: Right. [She develops the answer to give the class a much more detailed reply, contrasting the mother's situation in the story with their own lives.] Even though she's got all that work to do in the house, she's still very conscious of keeping herself clean and tidy. Because it's not just a case of taking off the apron, putting it in the washing machine, taking it out an hour later, spraying some starch on it, and that's the starched white apron. There's a lot of work involved. So, we know that the mother is a good, hard-working, caring woman.... Right, the turn of the father. What would you say about him?

The teacher goes on to discuss the presentation of the father in the story and pupils' responses to him in similar detail. At the conclusion of the phase, before she makes the transition to the next part of the lesson which will include pupils' own improvised scenes, she asks two final high order questions. How many of the class think that Billy (the boy in the story) was right to keep the money? And, what would they have done themselves if they had been in Billy's shoes? Both questions leave pupils 'on their own'; the answers lie 'in their heads' not in the text of the story. They offer lively and deeply felt responses, but discussion is much less focused and controlled at this point in the lesson.

In the course of this phase of the lesson, then, which has been examined in some detail, the teacher has drawn on and made use of most of the questioning techniques and strategies that have been identified and discussed earlier in the chapter. She has asked a wide range of questions at different levels of difficulty, some open, but most of them closed; she has directed questions to individuals, prompted and probed; she has encouraged and rewarded pupils when they have responded, and she has taken up their answers and developed them further, seeking to connect the subject-matter of the text to their existing experience and understanding. It is a controlled, clearly developed investigation taken at a brisk pace and with the pupils remaining interested and involved.

In conclusion, as in previous chapters, figure 7.1 presents a checklist of the qualities which are important to successful questioning techniques which have been described and discussed. Apart from acting as a summary of the chapter, the checklist can be used to help you to identify the strengths and weaknesses of your own classroom practice in this field.

Checklist of skills – questioning

ASKING QUESTIONS

Types of question

Did I indicate clearly which questions were open and which were closed?

Were my questions varied in nature and were they pitched at appropriate levels of difficulty?

Did I ask mostly low order questions requiring literal recall or recognition of information?

Did I also ask middle order questions requiring pupils to reorganise and apply information, infer and interpret?

Did I ask some high order questions requiring pupils to evaluate information or appreciate what had been achieved?

Were pupils aware of the appropriate resources they could draw on to answer the questions?

Did they realise that some answers were 'right there' in front of them? That for some they had to 'think and search' and for others they were 'on their own'?

Questioning strategies

Did I direct or redirect questions to specific pupils?

How did I select pupils to answer questions?

Did I offer prompts when pupils appeared to encounter difficulties?

Did I probe for more information, evidence or support when a reply was only partially satisfactory?

Responding

Did I encourage and reward pupils sufficiently when they answered questions?

Did I highlight particular aspects of pupils' answers?

Did I take up and develop further particular aspects of pupils' answers?

Did I attempt to make connections between pupils' answers and recently acquired or prior knowledge and experience?

Figure 7.1

Chapter eight

Evaluating your success as a teacher

The main body of this book has been about identifying, illustrating and discussing classroom skills in the teaching of English. In the opening chapter, however, I argued that initially at least it was also important to consider aims, purposes and values in the field of English teaching. This was because the beliefs you hold and the assumptions you make about the subject which is labelled 'English' on the curriculum, your own role in teaching it, and the ways in which children most effectively learn, will inevitably influence how you perceive and interpret the importance and usefulness of certain kinds of classroom skill. Similarly, in this concluding chapter, it again seems important to go beyond the accounts of different kinds of classroom skills that have been offered and consider how best you can set about evaluating or appraising your classroom performance after lessons have been implemented and the skills actually put into practice. If it is important, as I initially argued, for any teacher to possess a varied repertoire of professional skills which can be used in a range of contexts and for a variety of purposes, then it must be equally important to be able to identify what you seem to be doing well in a classroom, what you do less successfully (or not all), and the direction in which (for you at least) future development and improvement lie.

To attempt to appraise or evaluate your classroom practice without taking into account what your pupils appear to be learning, or their attitudes to you and the subject you teach, is clearly unacceptable. Teachers sometimes joke that their best lessons are taught when no children are there to distract them, but clearly, in reality, the sole purpose of your presence in any classroom and your continuing wish to master an increasing range of professional skills is to create opportunities for your pupils to learn effectively. Most of us would be disappointed if effective learning was not accompanied by some interest and enthusiasm on the part of at least some of our pupils towards ourselves as teachers and the content of the subject we teach. None the less, it would be foolhardy in the concluding chapter of a book of this nature to embark on a critical survey of the various methods and procedures that are available to you in your attempts to keep track of the progress your pupils are making in the entire field of the English curriculum. If you feel your expertise is lacking in this field and wish to explore it in more depth, suggestions for further reading are included in appendix A.

Instead, I intend to conclude by concentrating attention on the teacher in the classroom, as has been the case throughout the book, rather than on the children who are taught. And I shall consider the methods and procedures that are available to you in your attempts to keep track of your own progress and development as a teacher. In taking this approach I may appear to be condoning what is in fact an unacceptable divorce between the practice of teaching and the processes and outcomes of learning, but I believe none the less that the exploration is worth undertaking. Inevitably some of the questions I shall raise and some of the strategies I shall recommend can justifiably also be applied to the pupils themselves and the progress they in their turn are making through the curriculum, not merely to the teachers who are responsible for them.

Evaluating success – What are your purposes?

Assessment is not a universal or global term which can be applied in the same way to every person, topic or context. How you set about the task of making an evaluation of your teaching and the procedures you adopt are both likely to be influenced by a number of different factors – for instance, by the aims and purposes that lie behind the actual process of assessment, by the context in which the assessment will take place, and by the nature and number of individuals that are to be involved.

Let us at least start with the more familiar topic of assessing pupils' progress. Consider, for example, some of the possibilities that are open to you when you wish to assess your pupils' achievements and progress at different points in their school careers. You will obviously have very different aims and assessment purposes when:

   (i)   you return to a class a written assignment completed as part of
         a folder of course work;
  (ii)   you set some form of written test;
 (iii)   you enter a pupil as a candidate in an external or national
         examination.

In the first of these three examples, you will probably place uppermost your wish to convey to each pupil your response to what has been written, to identify and reinforce what has been done well, and to help the writer to develop and improve, possibly so that a second draft can be attempted. In the second example, though, you are likely to set a class or year-group test mainly to seek information about the current levels of achievement among different pupils in relation to their peers, and to discover what has been learned and retained as a result of your work together. In this case, you will probably simply add up the marks gained in different questions and produce a final order of merit. Almost certainly, because of the numbers and limited time involved, you will be able to provide much less in the way of information, or feedback, for individual pupils about what has been done well or badly. Entry in a public examination, on the other hand, will probably mark the completion of a course of study. The outcome will evaluate an individual's performance in relation to his or her peers nationally and will be used to select young people for work, for training, or for further education beyond school. In this last case individual pupils often receive no information about the nature of their achievements beyond the award of a final summarising grade or mark.

Similarly, when you are involved in appraising your own performance as a teacher (or contributing towards the appraisal of a colleague) some purposes are likely to be much more important than others. For example, you are likely to be interested, probably above all else, in identifying what your strengths and successes as a teacher are in order to increase your confidence and self-esteem. In other words, you will want to know what it is you do well. In addition, though, you should also be prepared to accept that you need to identify possible weaknesses in your performance so that you can set about doing something to overcome them. Generally speaking (and not surprisingly), teachers tend to be more resistant and defensive in this second area. Obviously we all find it much less palatable to be confronted by perceived lack of success and possible censure or rejection than to 'celebrate success'. This is why anxiety and often bitterness seem to underlie so many people's experiences and recollections of different forms of assessment at different points in their lives. Unfortunately, for many people school in particular seems to have been a place where as pupils they learned what they could *not* do, rather than a place where their talents (however slight) were recognised and encouraged to grow and where difficulties and impediments to learning were overcome.

In the same way, as a teacher working in a classroom, you will display individual talents that need to be recognised and encouraged. Your morale needs to be strengthened and your self-confidence increased. On the other hand, almost certainly, your performance is also likely to bring to light some weaknesses or difficulties (serious or trivial) that you will need help in overcoming. These may include, among other things, a lack of skill or expertise in a specific area of your teaching performance, or the complete absence of some identifiable skills or strategies from your professional repertoire. If this is the case, and you are advised to cover new ground and test out new approaches, you will almost certainly need help and continuing support. For it is obviously less demanding and stressful to attempt to improve and refine a mode of teaching which already appears to be working well than to develop your classroom practice in an entirely new direction.

On the other hand, few teachers, I suspect, would be interested in comparing themselves directly with others if this were to mean attempting to produce some kind of ranked order of professional merit. Any such list would in any case certainly lack validity. In attempting to draw one up, it would be difficult to take account of the different amounts and kinds of experience of the individuals involved. But more importantly, compiling such a list would assume that there does exist a large measure of agreement concerning what constitutes the most successful and the most effective way to teach. And no such consensus at present exists.

On the other hand, comparison with others, when it takes place on more neutral, less emotive ground, can be helpful and popular. In approaching comparison in these circumstances you are less likely to be concerned with deciding who is the better or less successful teacher (and if you are, you will tend to keep your judgements to yourself). You are much more interested in how a fellow practitioner copes in similar circumstances. There is a fascination in watching colleagues at work, in learning from their successes and difficulties, and in comparing with your own practice the ways in which (for example) they approach a class or topic, how they set up and organise a scheme of work, and how they handle recalcitrant pupils. After all, analysing how someone actually teaches and making comparisons between different kinds of practice are the only two feasible strategies available to you in any attempt to appraise and develop professional competence.

Probably selection is the only purpose which makes some kind of competitive comparison between teachers acceptable. For example, outstanding classroom performance may well be an important criterion for promotion or career advancement, or for a teacher's involvement in teacher training or programmes of staff induction or development. Under such circumstances (as I shall argue in more detail later, see page 158) it seems essential to base selection on accepted procedures, on agreed criteria, and on explicit evidence. Traditionally, in many departments and schools, senior teachers claim that they can accurately predict who their outstanding teachers are, but often appear much less assured if challenged about the grounds for their choice or the evidence on which it is founded. And beginning teachers are sometimes justifiably bitter about reports written about them which attempt to define the level of competence they have reached and the progress they are making, when little apparent effort has been made either to observe them at work in a classroom or to discuss their development with them.

A final important purpose of appraisal, therefore, is to set standards or benchmarks for satisfactory minimum levels of classroom competence. Although such benchmarks are essential for judging and validating the performance of beginning teachers, they can clearly be of importance at any point in a teacher's career, especially when doubts about an individual's competence are consistently voiced from a variety of sources. Again, it seems essential that the enforcing of such standards should rest on agreed procedures and accepted criteria, and for decisions to be reached only after carefully considering explicit and agreed evidence.

Procedures for evaluation

There are two ways of approaching the process of professional evaluation – either you accept the main responsibility for undertaking it yourself, or a more experienced colleague (or outsider) will undertake the process for you. As I have suggested throughout this book, the two approaches are not incompatible. You can accept responsibility for the evaluation of your own teaching yourself and you can in addition work in collaboration with another colleague to help and learn from each other. But although it is possible to adopt different perspectives or viewpoints on appraisal, there must inevitably be significant differences in the amount of time and effort that can be allocated to it. In a sense, self-evaluation can and should be a constant and continuous process. External appraisal, on the other hand, whether it takes the form of a co-operative enterprise or is an imposed requirement, must necessarily be occasional or 'periodic' and is likely to be concentrated in form and intensity.

Self-evaluation, then, is likely to be continuous and informal in nature. I have already argued that when you are teaching in a classroom you should accept that you need to be constantly alert to the behaviour of your class, watching and listening, picking up cues and signals about their progress on a task, and making judgements about the skills individual pupils possess and the abilities they manifest. Similarly, before, during and especially after a lesson, you should also be constantly questioning the goals you have set for a lesson, the teaching approaches and materials you have chosen, the decisions you take and the skills you call upon as you teach, and the ways in which you interact with and manage your classes. To meet such demands is challenging. Teaching, even in its simplest forms, is complex and can be stressful. As I indicated in the opening pages of this book, it is easy to experience a warm glow of satisfaction when a lesson goes well, or a deep sense of pessimism and dissatisfaction when things go badly. A major purpose of the intervening chapters has been to make explicit the complex skills of different modes of classroom teaching and to provide you with a firmer and more coherent framework for analysis and evaluation. The discussion and exemplification that have been provided should have helped you to identify more confidently and accurately the qualities that have helped to make any lesson you teach successful or unsatisfactory, and to suggest possible reasons for these outcomes. If this is the case, you will be able to take action in future to capitalise on your strengths and compensate for or overcome your weaknesses as a teacher.

The most effective and most demanding form of appraisal, then, should be self-appraisal. And, as a result, you should be able to make the judgements and decisions you reach explicit and available to any out-sider. If, on the other hand, you are collaborating with a colleague, your relationship and the procedures you adopt can still remain informal. For many years teachers have successfully 'team-taught' with colleagues in their own department or related subject fields to explore a theme together and pool resources, to create larger groups of pupils than occur in a conventional class (to show, for example, a video or film), and to enable smaller groups of pupils to be formed for intensive remedial support. The notion of 'co-operative' teaching is similar, but normally entails a specialist remedial or 'learning support' teacher working alongside the main subject-teacher and giving additional help to any child who needs it. Both approaches create valuable opportunities for teachers to learn from each other, but obviously their main purpose is to develop the quality of classroom teaching and learning as experienced by the pupils, rather than to appraise and develop the skills of the teachers concerned. The most helpful collaborative strategy directed explicitly towards professional development is 'peer coaching'. Here an inexperienced teacher is deliberately paired with an appropriate more experienced colleague and over a short, concentrated period of time, they are timetabled to share each others' classrooms, to plan, teach and evaluate work together. The benefits that this approach provides are by no means one-sided; experienced teachers can learn as much from the process as their less experienced colleagues.

The most obvious and persistent constraints on such collaborative approaches to professional evaluation and development are the admin-istrative problems involved in arranging them, and, more importantly, the apparent lack of available time within the school day. This lack of time – the teacher's most precious resource – is especially critical when it comes to arranging opportunities for the team to plan and evaluate work together, in particular to exchange ideas about what happened in shared lessons, to discuss what each believes was achieved and the difficulties that were encountered.

The least effective and most anxiety-provoking approach to appraisal is undoubtedly the set-piece lesson. Such lessons tend to be over-prepared by the teacher and to be observed by an unfamiliar, senior, or external assessor. Neither teacher nor pupils usually behave in character, the assessor possesses few shared understandings about the context or purposes of the lesson, and any discussion that follows is likely to be stilted and general in nature. There may be occasions in a teacher's career when such a 'driving test' approach to evaluation is essential, but they are unlikely to be productive as far as the development of the assessed teacher is concerned and they should be few and far between.

Obviously the most appropriate evidence on which to base evaluation and discussion is the content and methods of actual lessons that have been observed or team-taught. This kind of experiential evidence can be supported (and shared with others) by making audio- and especially video-recordings of lessons. Audio-recordings can offer helpful but limited insights into a lesson's strengths and weaknesses. Such recordings are probably best used only for individual self-evaluation rather than joint discussions and they can help you to recall how a lesson developed or to examine in some detail a particular phase of a lesson, especially your own behaviour in it. Recordings can be made with simple equipment which can either be left in a fixed position in the classroom or can be moved round as the lesson develops. If you use this method, it is usually possible to record the teacher's voice to an acceptable standard, but it is more difficult to pick up clearly the voices of some pupils.

Video-recording lessons, on the other hand, is more difficult to arrange, but the results are more interesting and stimulate much more critical discussion. A camera with built-in microphone and a video-recorder can be set up in a fixed position at the back of a room and set running at the start of a lesson until its conclusion, with acceptable, but sometimes frustrating results. Obviously you cannot guarantee that either teacher or pupils will stay 'in frame'. Ideally the camera is best worked by a collaborating teacher (although this makes it more difficult to work together during the lesson) or possibly by a senior pupil or technician in the school. The children actually involved in the lesson usually quickly accept the presence of the camera once some of them have got over an initial bid for attention. Much of the exemplar material used in earlier chapters was acquired in this way with teachers video-recording their own lessons for use in later discussions. Sometimes these recordings were made by the teachers themselves working on their own, and sometimes they were assisted by a colleague, senior pupil or technician.

Finally, it is worth reflecting on the possibility of a hidden agenda or hidden curriculum for assessment in this field. In one small-scale investigation, for example, beginning teachers reported on the anxiety that was caused by the pressures created by external informal assessment in their probationary years. Senior teachers, they claimed, tended to come into their classrooms unannounced, ostensibly to pick up books or teaching materials, but clearly also wishing to make a quick evaluation of the teacher's progress. And on other more formal occasions, like at staff or departmental meetings, the probationers also felt that their contributions to discussion were likely to influence other teachers' perceptions of their overall professional competence (Cuthbert 1987).

The nature and processes of evaluation

In the field of professional development there should be no attempt to offer a definitive, final or 'summative' evaluation. As I argued in the opening chapter, we are all of us learning to teach all our lives (or should be). There may be important staging points in a teacher's career – when you first enter the profession, for example, and complete your period as a probationary teacher, or when you are considered for different kinds of advancement or promotion – but the processes of professional development and the guidance and support you are offered should continue throughout your career. It follows, therefore, that assessment should be partly summative in nature (at the conclusion of particular career phases), but in the main, and more importantly, it should be 'formative'.

Formative assessment aims to help shape or develop behaviour. As a teacher yourself, working with pupils, you are constantly involved in the processes of formative assessment, both informally when you respond to children in class and try to help them to understand or do something better, and more formally when you read what they have written and try to help them to improve. Formative assessment, then, is 'diagnostic' in the sense that you seek to identify the strengths and weaknesses of a person's performance and take appropriate action to help them to improve. Sometimes, in addition, it is possible to surmise why a difficulty is being experienced and how a problem has come about, but obviously time is limited and it is rarely possible to investigate such difficulties in detail and depth. You tend to have to take the evidence at face value and do the best you can to help the person concerned to make progress and improve.

You can, of course, as I have already indicated, be your own assessor. You can leave your classroom and hasten to a refuge or sanctuary elsewhere in the school to think coolly and critically about the lesson you have just taught. You can ask yourself what went well and what was less successful (or disastrous). You can reflect on the reasons particularly for your difficulties and failures and think about what you would do to improve the lesson if you were to teach it again. But normally formative assessment is a joint venture. It presupposes some-one – the assessor – with more experience and greater professional expertise working with the person who is to be assessed. Their principal objective is to identify the strengths and weaknesses in that second person's performance and to share in the processes of improvement and development.

The relationship between the assessor and the person to be assessed is always sensitive and delicate. Unfortunately, in the circumstances we are considering, teachers' professional instincts often seem to encourage them to be overwhelmingly destructive and negative in their approach to the task, in much the same way that many teachers still approach the assessment of pupils' work negatively. It is often easy to see what is being done badly or has gone wrong, and to take for granted what is being done well or has been successful. Many teachers, too, when they act as appraisers tend to accept a traditional didactic role and simply transmit or relay information to the person being assessed. There is often little sense of dialogue or an exchange of views.

The first main thrust of assessment, then, needs to be positive and encouraging to build up the confidence and self-esteem of the person whose work is being appraised. Your starting point should always be the successes of a lesson and what went well, not to give immediate attention to what went wrong. But the assessor also needs to be a good listener. If you take on the role, you should encourage your 'clients', like any good teacher in a classroom, to ask their own questions and come to their own conclusions about the lessons they have taught. Dialogue and response are obviously much more demanding of your interpersonal skills and your time, but the end results seem to be much more valuable and satisfying for the people concerned. The teachers being appraised will then create their own agenda for the discussions and make their own connections with earlier experiences. Your own role will be more to listen, question, respond and guide, than to direct and inform. It is comparatively easy, as we have already indicated, to tell people quickly and concisely what went well in a particular lesson and what went wrong, and to give advice about how they could be more proficient. It is more difficult but in the long term more effective to create a climate where the teachers being assessed are ready to listen and to participate in a constructive debate about how they might improve.

Many teachers of English in their day-to-day work appear to adopt a 'flotation' approach to the process of assessment. And they seem to respond holistically rather than analytically to whatever is to be assessed. That is, they first like to experience classroom phenomena as a 'whole' in a particular context rather than begin by selecting and organising particular aspects of an experience for detailed attention. Once they have taken in this first overall impression, they then allow particular aspects to 'float' to the surface of their consciousness for detailed consideration and discussion. For example, when they have set some kind of extended writing task for pupils to complete, and begin to assess what has been written, they like to view each script as a unity, not as a collection of discrete parts. And as they read, they will allow what appear to them to be the distinctive features or qualities of that unity (good and bad) to 'float' into their conscious minds. These features or qualities (the ability to tell a story, for instance, or appropriate choice of descriptive vocabulary, or accuracy of spelling) will then form the subject-matter for the responses and evaluations they will make about what has been written (Peacock 1986: 52–3).

A classroom lesson must clearly also be regarded as a totality or 'whole'. Like a piece of extended writing, it is a complex unity of different elements which interconnect and interrelate. Few teachers of English seem to find it helpful to concentrate discussion on one particular aspect of a lesson – the questions you asked, for example, or the explanations you gave. In a sense, then, assessment does need to be holistic, because you need to be concerned with the success of the lesson as a whole. But it does not follow that holistic assessment must be only 'global' in the kinds of judgements and responses you offer ('That was a good lesson', for instance). The total experience of the lesson has to be broken down into manageable components so that you can consider each in some detail in order to work towards specific improvements.

In order to bring about an appropriate balance between an overview of the context, purposes and development of the whole lesson, and the analysis of specific features or phases within it, both assessor and assessed ideally need to share a common conceptual framework and descriptive vocabulary about the nature of teaching (both of which have been offered in this book). If this is the case, the process of assessment can be given a clearer sense of direction and become more systematic. This is not to say that its form must necessarily become authoritarian, impersonal or mechanistic, as many teachers of English seem immediately to assume. Assessment can remain informal, open, and flexible. You can approach the task in many different ways and from a variety of directions and starting points. But you will have an agreed and defined agenda, all or part of which you can cover (in any order) in the course of your discussions. For example, very few of the teachers who have had access to the checklists provided in earlier chapters have worked through these systematically, item by item. They have been regarded more as a resource and a series of maps of the territory to be covered than as an agenda to be strictly followed. You can refer to the checklists and make use of them in any way that seems helpful or appropriate. In short, your shared approach to the task of assessment needs to be systematic and analytic, but your analyses should not lose sight either of the total context in which your teaching takes place or how the different parts of a particular lesson relate to each other.

If, then, evaluation or appraisal needs in the main to be formative and analytic in approach, and if your main purpose is to identify strengths and weaknesses in your own or another teacher's performance rather than simply to label or grade teachers as good, bad or indifferent, it follows that the procedures you follow for assessment must be criterion-referenced rather than norm-referenced. If, for instance, your approach to assessment were to be norm-referenced, you would wish to establish some kind of 'norm' of agreed good professional practice and then evaluate each teacher's classroom performance in terms of whether it corresponded to this notional general benchmark or was better or worse. It would be an effective procedure for distinguishing between teachers and, if necessary, labelling or grading them. For example, the performance of an assessed C-grade teacher would correspond to the norms expected, whereas (on a five point scale) teachers labelled A or B would be outstanding or above average, and those graded D or E would be considered poor or incompetent. I have, however, argued earlier in this chapter that it would be difficult to achieve any consensus within the profession as a whole about what would 'count' in deciding on the benchmarks used to define acceptable standards of professional competence. Values, beliefs and purposes in the teaching of English are too varied and commitments too strong. And in any case, most people would find it unacceptable and offensive to label or grade teachers in this way (even if only at staging posts in their careers).

Criterion-referenced assessment, on the other hand, demands that you must first make clear and explicit what it is you are trying to achieve. Then you must try to make equally clear what will 'count' as evidence of success so that you can be confident that you have actually attained your goals. The 'criteria' in criterion-referenced assessment are the qualities you will be explicitly looking for in judging any successful performance. In these circumstances, 'success' should be thought of not in terms of a graduated scale – satisfactory, good, very good, or outstanding (terms associated with norm-referenced assessment) – but rather on a single 'Yes/No' dimension. Either something has been done satisfactorily and you have met a particular criterion or set of criteria – you are confident that the qualities you are looking for are clearly present – or your performance has in some way been unsatisfactory – in which case you will need help and support before you try again.

In other words, given the criteria for success you have set yourself or have agreed on for evaluating your teaching performance, you will have to ask yourself (or ask jointly with another collaborating teacher) whether you have reached acceptable professional standards in planning, preparing and implementing your lesson. Or, to be more down-to-earth, you will have to ask yourself, after teaching a lesson, what it was you were trying to achieve, how you had proposed to achieve it, and whether or not you have been successful. If you believe that your success in teaching the lesson has been complete, can you justify this judgement? If, on the other hand, you believe your lesson has been only partially successful (which is more likely), or that the lesson has failed completely (which is rare), what evidence would you offer to illustrate your dissatisfaction or sense of failure? And what action do you propose to take in order to raise the unsatisfactory features of the lesson to an acceptable standard?

What will count as success?

I argued in the opening chapter that the teaching of English should not be 'assessment-led' or dominated by assessment objectives. Instead, in your role as teacher, you should begin by making explicit and clear to yourself and your classes what it is you are trying to achieve, both in the long term (over the course of a school year and beyond), and in the shorter term when you are more concerned with a particular unit of work or sequence of lessons. It is only when you have produced this statement of goals that you should be prepared to select limited targets for assessment and choose procedures that are appropriate to your purposes in monitoring the progress that has been made and evaluating what has been achieved.

If, on the other hand, your teaching is directed towards and dominated by pre-selected and often isolated assessment targets, the experiences and the opportunities you offer to your pupils are likely to be limiting and narrow. A checklist of assessment targets can provide a useful and helpful overview or map of the ground that has to be covered in an English course, but it is you, the teacher, working in a particular context, who must decide what the priorities are, how different aspects of the course interrelate, and which route you and your pupils are to take.

The same is true of the evaluation of your own performance as a teacher. It is again you, the teacher, who must take the initiative in trying to make clear what you are trying to achieve, the methods and resources you are using in order to attain your goals, and how you have decided to organise your classroom and manage your classes. You must try to articulate what will count as success for you, at this given point in your professional career, and the difficulties and frustrations you are experiencing in the progress you are making towards your goals. Needless to say, not all teachers will perceive success in the same way, nor will they encounter the same problems. In such differences lie opportunities for continuing discussion and improved understanding.

In this concluding section, therefore, you are not to be offered a definitive analysis of the diverse elements which constitute 'success' in any appraisal of a teacher's classroom performance. Instead, as suggested earlier, you will be offered a map which attempts to chart the territory and identifies important landmarks to help you to find your best route through it. You will discover few surprises when you see what is being offered. The terminology is straightforward and the categories and supporting examples have been drawn up in consultation with experienced, practising teachers of English. The subject-matter is arranged to some extent in a chronological sequence to follow the planning, implementation and evaluation of a single lesson or unit of work, but the categories that are used can be discussed in any order and connections can be readily made between the categories. Once the map has become familiar to you through use, its contents and structure should become part of your habitual thinking about the nature of teaching. If so, its job will have been done and its usefulness will be over.

The framework that is being offered for appraising or evaluating your success as a teacher comprises the following categories:

Aims and knowledge of course content
Can you (for example) make explicit and clear what it is you are trying to achieve as a teacher of English?
Can you discuss clearly and confidently what your goals are in teaching individual lessons or a sequence of lessons?
Do you possess good knowledge of texts and other resources appropriate to classroom use?
Do you possess good knowledge of the English curriculum prescribed by the school and the requirements for external examinations?

Planning and preparation
Can you choose successful themes or 'organising centres' for lessons or units of work?
Can you select and if necessary create appropriate and successful resource materials?
Can you devise tasks at appropriate levels of difficulty?
Can you successfully plan and sequence appropriate phases in the development of a lesson?
Do you prepare additional associated tasks and assignments (such as optional extensions to core tasks or homework)?
Do you consider alternatives in case things go wrong?

Teaching methods
Do you make appropriate use of different modes of teaching?
Do you implement different modes with confidence and skill?

(See also the detailed checklists for directive, discursive, inquiry and activity approaches: figures 2.1, 3.1, 4.1, 5.1.)

Communicating effectively in the classroom

Do you use your voice effectively? (Can you be heard? Do you vary your voice in volume, pace, and expression?)

Do you read aloud with expression and skill?

Is the language you use appropriate to the classes you teach (in vocabulary and sentence construction)?

Are your explanations and instructions clear?

Is your questioning skilled and productive?

Do you make effective use of the blackboard and other audio-visual aids?

(See also the detailed checklists on explaining and asking questions: figures 6.1, 7.1.)

Relationships with pupils

Do you relate easily to pupils of different ages?

Are you sensitive to pupils' own interests?

Do you readily accept pupils' contributions to lessons?

Do you encourage and 'reward' pupils sufficiently?

Classroom management

Do you establish a purposeful 'climate' for learning?

Are the rules that operate in your classroom clear and explicit?

Do you begin and end lessons with authority and confidence?

Do you manage classroom routines effectively (such as seating arrangements, and giving out books or materials)?

Are the transitions you make between phases in a lesson smooth and clearly 'signalled'?

Do you get flustered when you have to deal with two or more matters simultaneously?

Do you pace lessons successfully and manage time effectively?

Classroom control

Do you successfully monitor the behaviour of the whole class throughout a lesson (in all its phases)?

Are your expectations as regards pupils' standards of work and behaviour high enough (or too high)?

Are you able to anticipate behaviour problems and prevent them escalating? (Do you intervene too soon or too late?)

Do you welcome or avoid confrontations with individuals?

Do you deal with behaviour problems firmly and fairly?

When necessary, do you make effective use of the sanctions available to you (through school or department policy)?

Assessment

Do you manage to keep track of pupils' progress informally while they are actually at work in class (when completing a writing task, or contributing to a discussion, for instance)?

Do you keep more formal records to summarise pupils' progress and achievements? How detailed and effective are these?

When you mark written work, are you confident about your own standards in judging what has been achieved?

Do you make your criteria for assessment clear to pupils?

Do you respond positively to pupils' work?

Do you also identify what is less successful or causing problems and help them to improve?

Do you have a good grasp of school policies for assessment and the requirements of externally assessed courses?

Are you self-critical about your own teaching, open to advice, and willing to learn?

It is a daunting and demanding agenda (and you will probably want to make your own further additions to it). No one should argue that teaching children or young people in a classroom is simple or easy. But rest assured, if you are now beginning your career as a teacher, the first five years are likely to prove the most difficult (and the first two the most difficult of all), and by the time you have mastered all the skills that are expected of you, you will probably be more than ready for the solace of a quiet retirement.

Appendix A

Selected recommended reading

Aims in the teaching of English

Abbs, P. (1982) *English within the arts: a radical alternative for English and the arts in the curriculum*, Hodder & Stoughton, London.

Allen, D. (1988) *English, whose English?*, National Association of Advisers in English/National Association for the Teaching of English (NATE), Sheffield.

Blanchard, J. (1986) *Out in the open: a secondary English curriculum*, Cambridge University Press, Cambridge.

Department of Education and Science (1986) *English from 5 to 16: curriculum matters I*, 2nd edn, HMSO, London.

—— (1988) *English from ages 5 to 16: proposals of the Secretary of State for Education and Science*, National Curriculum Council, London.

—— (1988) *Report of the committee of inquiry into the teaching of English language (The Kingman report)*, HMSO, London.

Evans, T. (1982) *Teaching English*, Croom Helm, London.

Gatherer, W.A. (1980) *A study of English: learning and teaching the language*, Heinemann Educational, London.

Harrison, B.T. (ed.) (1983) *English Studies 11–18: an arts based approach*, Hodder & Stoughton, London.

Holbrook, D. (1979) *English for meaning*, NFER, Windsor.

Keen, J. (1978) *Teaching English: a linguistic approach*, Methuen, London.

Marenbon, J. (1987) *English our English: the new orthodoxy examined*, Centre for Policy Studies, London.

Mathieson, M. (1975) *The preachers of culture: a study of English and its teachers*, Allen & Unwin, London.

Paffard, M. (1978) *Thinking about English*, Ward Lock Educational, London.

Watson, K. (1987) *English teaching in perspective*, revised edn, Open University Press, Milton Keynes.

Resources

Jackson, D. (1982) *Continuity in secondary English*, Methuen, London.
Mills, R.W. (1987) *Teaching English to all*, 2nd edn, Robert Royce, London.
Protherough, R., Atkinson, J., and Fawcett, J. (1989) *The effective teaching of English*, (chapter 4), Longman, London.

Assessment in the teaching of English

Black, H. and Broadfoot, P. (1982) *Keeping track of teaching: assessment in the modern classroom*, Routledge, London.
Brown, S. (1981) *What do they know? A review of criterion- referenced assessment*, HMSO, Edinburgh.
Chater, P. (1984) *Marking and assessment in English*, Methuen, London.
Dunsbee, T. (1980) *Mark my words: a study of teachers as correctors of children's writing*, Ward Lock Educational/NATE, London.
Rowntree, D. (1987) *Assessing students: how shall we know them?*, revised edn, Kegan Page, London.
Stibbs, A. (1979) *Assessing children's language: guidelines for teachers*, Ward Lock Educational/NATE, London.

Appendix B

The characteristics of the short story

1. The writer must express himself in a minimum of words. This means that there is no place for lengthy introductions or elaborate picturing of background which are found so often in the novel. The climax is at or very near the end of the story. The story closes as soon as its purpose has been accomplished.
2. The short story can introduce only a few characters to the reader. It generally contains at least two characters, for conflict, but usually the emphasis is on one. No character is introduced who is not absolutely necessary. Lack of space prevents any attempt at full development of character; we must be content with the portrayal of a crisis in a character's life, and with a few easily remembered traits. A good short story writer gives us quick pen-portraits, drawn economically, yet with individuality.
3. Although every short story has three basic elements – setting, characterisation, and action – only one is emphasised in each story. Because the short story has to move rapidly, the opening paragraph (often the first sentence) informs the reader which of the above elements will play the most important part.
4. The plot is never complicated but it may contain surprises. These surprises should be unexpected, but perfectly acceptable in the light of what has gone before.
5. There is no place in the short story for lengthy description or for the author's personal observations.
6. To produce the single effect planned by the author, the short story should be capable of being read at one sitting.
7. The short story frequently has unity of time, place and action. This is especially true of place because frequent changes of scene destroy the unity of impression basic to the short story.

To summarise, a short story is fictional prose writing characterised by:

brevity;
compression;
unity of impression;
a technique involving a direct opening, rapid and unimpeded action, and a logical conclusion.

Seatbelts in cars

1. Appoint a chairperson and secretary to your group.
2. As you will know, all people who travel in the front seats of
   cars must (by law) wear a safety belt. It is likely that in the near
   future all children (and perhaps all adults too) will have to wear
   safety belts when they travel in the back seats of cars. Read the
   press cutting printed below:

SUCCESS IS LIKELY FOR SEATBELTS BILL

A bill to make it compulsory for children to wear seatbelts in the back
of cars is to be introduced in the Commons and is likely to be enacted.

Mr Stephen Day, the Tory MP who came fifth in the ballot for
private members' Bills, said yesterday that his Bill had all-party
support and the backing of such organisations as the RAC, the
Association of Chief Police Officers, the Casualty Surgeons'
Association and the Child Accident Prevention Trust. It is also
viewed favourably by the Government.

The Bill would apply only to children of 13 and under, and to
drivers whose cars are fitted with rear seatbelts. However, since April
1st this year all new cars have had to have such belts.

Mr Day, MP for Cheadle, believes that his measure would reduce
child fatalities and injuries by at least three-quarters. At present only
31 per cent of children wear rear seatbelts.

Last year, 89 per cent injured in road accidents were seated in the
back and 91 per cent of those killed.

Similar legislation already exists in Australia, Canada, the United
States and the Netherlands.

Martin Fletcher, *The Times*, 23rd October 1987

3. Discuss in your group the advantages and disadvantages that
   any new law about wearing safety belts in the rear seats of cars
   would bring. The secretary should make a list of the advantages
   and disadvantages suggested.

4. Next read the off-print headed, 'Family trapped under water after car crash are rescued.' Then discuss in your group whether the information you have just been given changes any of the conclusions you have reached.
5. Finally, read the article, 'Safety belts – could this happen to you?' Then discuss whether this new information affects any of the conclusions you have reached.
6. The secretary will present a report on your group's conclusions to the whole class.

Appendix D

'The Werewolf Strikes Again'

It was the Saturday of a weekend patrol camp and after the evening meal I idly asked the boys what they wanted to do. I should have known better. The spokesman for the party turned to me and said, 'Well, we were hoping you would ask that. You see there's a film show on tonight. We thought we might go – if it's all right with you.'

The thought of warm, plush seats in a draught-free hall appealed to me greatly and by half-past seven we had washed, changed, and were tramping into the cinema.

As soon as the title flashed across the screen I knew I had made a fatal mistake. Sinister growls, a couple of spine-chilling shrieks, and there it was in letters a foot high, *The Werewolf Strikes Again!*

For the next 90 minutes slaughter piled upon slaughter. I lost count after the fifth victim had been devoured by the rampaging monster, but still death followed death.

By the time we left the cinema the eyes of the rest were popping from their heads, and I must confess even I was feeling more than a little nervous as we struck out through the darkness back to Long Meadow Farm.

Hurrying past the old churchyard where tombstones glistened ghostly white in the chasing beams of a pale moon, we left the main road and headed towards the sombre mass of Twelve Oaks Spinney. As we crossed a silent meadow someone spoke. 'Hey, men, imagine meeting the werewolf now!'

Another said nervously, 'Shut up! It's spooky enough without you reminding us of that film.'

He was right. The high-riding moon was playing hide-and-seek with banks of woolly cloud, and thick shadows clung to every bush and tree, causing them to assume weird shapes as they loomed above us out of the night.

171

We squeezed through a narrow gate in the high hedgerow, and I had just turned to re-fasten the catch when someone let out a yell. 'What on earth?...' I spun round on my heel. White-faced he pointed to his right. A huge black mass was emerging slowly from the shadows. Silently it advanced towards us as we trembled by the gateway. Each ponderous step the object made, we retreated. Then suddenly it stopped. We waited. For a second time stood still. Then someone burst out laughing.

'Crikey, fellows, it's only an old cow.'

At the sound of his voice, the beast swung her head, mooing softly, as we sheepishly filed around her. Laughing and joking about our fears, we crossed the field and plunged into the wood. Immediately our chatter ceased. Beneath the waving branches the air was cold and dank. A thin mist hung in luminous patches over the dense undergrowth and our pace was reduced to a crawl as we struggled to keep to the winding pathway which was hidden in the thick darkness.

Deeper and deeper into the wood we stumbled, and I was thinking we had lost our way, when suddenly we heard a noise. Louder and louder it drifted eerily through the night air. A low, coughing, yelping howl which crept nearer and nearer with every second that passed.

'Cripes, what's that?' someone said.

'Search me,' I replied. 'But I don't like it!'

Suddenly a shadowy form broke noisily from the undergrowth and hurtled into the darkness some 20 yards from where we were standing. Eyes glinting red in the cold moonlight, long tongue dangling over wicked fang, the beast slipped silently from our view.

'You don't believe...?' I was just about to scold him when the air about us sang with a fearful howling. The hairs on my head literally tingled and I was conscious of a heavy, musty scent which seemed to be rising in clouds from the very ground on which we stood. I shivered despite myself, and I heard someone whisper in my ear, 'You've smelled 'em too? Remember the film?'

I remembered. The scent of a werewolf is the last thing his victim is ever conscious of. Rooted to the spot I waited. Crashing through the bushes a flood of fearsome beasts padded softly into the tiny clearing. Their breath rising in great clouds of steam, saliva drooling from each powerful jaw, they raced and chased about our leaden feet – werewolves! At that moment I was ready to believe all the films and comics.

Round and round the pack circled, their fierce yelpings ringing and pounding in our ears until it seemed as if we must be drowned in the maelstrom of whirling, plunging bodies.

Suddenly, loud and clear above the snapping clamour of the beasts, came the sound of a high-pitched whistle. With one accord the pack halted, swerved, and streamed away into the darkness in a welter of legs and tails.

As the noise of their passage died away in the night, a white-faced person shattered the silence. 'I'm off!' and he crashed blindly through the undergrowth in headlong flight. The rest of us were not far behind. Tripping and stumbling we fled from the clearing, twisting and turning through the shadows, the noise of those infernal beasts still ringing in our ears.

I don't know how we reached the camp site, but I do remember that we spent all night shivering in the tent with our sleeping bags pulled tight above our heads.

We never did find out what they were and where that whistle came from.

Malcolm (aged 13 years)

Appendix E

Holidays

Worksheet 1 Booking a holiday

1. Decide on who makes up the family unit – with names and ages (up to four people). For example, a young couple and baby, a retired couple and dog, etc.

Names: *Age:*

(i)   ....

(ii) ....

(iii) ....

(iv) ....

2. Decide what sort of holiday, for example, seaside, climbing, scenic, activity (golf, pony-trekking).

....

....

3. Decide on the questions to ask before you make the booking – for example, seasonal changes, price concessions, number of rooms, length of stay, facilities offered.

....

....

4. Make the call

Worksheet 2 Wish you were here?

Hotel Paloma Blanca

A few miles west of the town, but enjoying a superb location in a quiet bay, this 200-bedroomed hotel is superbly equipped with private bathrooms and with television and coffee-making facilities in all bedrooms. Swimming pools, palm-fringed gardens and comfortable bars make this an ideal hotel for a relaxing holiday. Amenities include:

- two full-sized swimming pools, one for children
- two lounge bars open all day
- El Rocko disco with sound and laser effects
- restaurant and Spanish bar
- games room
- well-maintained gardens
- video shows twice a week
- baby-sitting service

Fred Smith's Letter

Dear Sir

I am writing to complain about a holiday which I had recently at the Hotel Paloma Blanca. Several points in the brochure description were inaccurate.

Firstly, the hotel was 20 miles from the town and overlooked a smelly, noisy fishmarket. The bedroom was shabby and the television failed to work. The swimming pools were crowded and the bars were full of Germans singing and swigging beer. The restaurants were grossly overpriced and the food was revolting.

My principal complaint is about the noise. The disco was directly below our rooms and even though we repeatedly complained to the manager, we were unable to obtain a different room or a lessening of noise.

I feel very strongly that your brochure gave a false view of what the hotel was like and request that some compensation be made for the discomfort we suffered.

Yours faithfully

Task

1. In groups form a company of travel agents and consider Fred's letter:

How many of his complaints are the company's fault?
How many are the hotel's fault?
How many are outside anyone's control (e.g. bad luck)?
Will the company give any compensation? If so, how much?

Take notes and be prepared to report back to the rest of the class.

2. Using these notes, write a letter to Fred Smith, stating the company's policy and the decisions you have reached.

'The Great Escape'

Confidential dossier

Name of the group: The Commandos

Names of group members:
1. Rambo (Lindsay)
2. Fred (Tommy)
3. Sarge (Matthew)
4. Scotty (Duncan)
5. ....
(Overleaf each group member should state how he was captured.)

Name of spokesman: Scotty (Duncan)

Camp layout: The camp is enclosed in a barbed wire fence with a trip-wire close to the inside of it. There are two fences, 12 feet high, each 6 feet apart, and the space in the middle is filled with coiled barbed wire. There is a small gate. There are 10 barracks with corridors joining them.

Camp organisation: At night savage dogs roam corridors. Ferrets (spies) search the place. Our stooges try to follow them. There is an escape committee which gives you help and information.

Camp plan: draw a plan of the camp on the attached sheet. In addition to details mentioned by the senior British officer, include cookhouse and latrines and mark your barracks.

Escape plan

Brief outline of plan:
We will hang-glide out of the camp using a decoy in which the guards will be told of a plan to escape by an anonymous informer. While they are looking for the fake attempt to escape we will glide away and land miles away.

Equipment and materials needed and how these will be obtained: Metal or wooden poles, jubilee clips or strong twine, cotton sheet, better nylon sheets. Small gun and dagger. Radio. Paint.

Assistance required:
Decoy informer.

Problem areas:
How to test the hang-glider.

Reasons for thinking your plan will succeed:
The reasons we think the plan will succeed are it is completely novel and they don't expect it.

References

Asimov, I. (1978) 'The fun they had', in J. Gibson (ed.) *Science Fiction*, John Murray, London.

Bradbury, R. (ed. Adams A.) (1975) *Ray Bradbury*, Harrap (Pegasus Library), London.

Brown, G., Anderson, A., Shillcock, R., and Yule, G. (1984) *Teaching talk: strategies for production and assessment*, Cambridge University Press, Cambridge.

Brown, G.A. and Armstrong, S. (1984) 'Explaining and explanations', in E.C. Wragg (ed.) *Classroom teaching skills: the research findings of the Teacher Education project*, Croom Helm, London.

Brown, G.A. and Edmondson, R. (1984) 'Asking questions', in E.C. Wragg, (ed.) *Classroom teaching skills: the research findings of the Teacher Education project*, Croom Helm, London.

Cuthbert, T.P. (1987) 'The probationary teacher in the Scottish secondary school: a study of assessment and support', unpublished M.Ed. dissertation, University of Stirling.

Department of Education and Science (1988) *English for ages 5 to 11: proposals of the Secretary of State for Education and Science and the Secretary of State for Wales*, National Curriculum Council, London.

Dunkin, M.J. and Biddle, B.J. (1974) *The study of teaching*, Holt, Rinehart and Winston, New York.

Edwards, R. (1972) 'Hero in the dust', in M. Marland (ed.) *Scene scripts*, Longmans, London.

Graves, R. (1959) *Collected poems 1959*, Cassell, London.

Halward, L. (1965) 'The Breadwinner', in J.C. Reid (ed.) *Forty short short stories*, Edward Arnold, London.

Hargreaves, D.H., Hester, S.K., and Mellor, F.J. (1975) *Deviance in classrooms*, Routledge, London.

Heaney, S. (1980) *Selected poems 1965–1975*, Faber, London.

Hines, B. (1968) *A kestrel for a knave (Kes)*, Penguin Books, Harmondsworth.

Hughes, R. (1988) 'A night at a cottage', in *The dragon's head: classic English short stories*, Oxford University Press, Oxford.

Jacobs, W.W. (1978) 'The monkey's paw' in J. Gibson and A. Ridout (eds) *Supernatural*, John Murray, London.

Kerry, T. (1984) 'Analysing the cognitive demand made by classroom tasks in mixed-ability classes', in E.C.Wragg (ed.) *Classroom teaching skills: the research findings of the Teacher Education project*, Croom Helm, London.
—— (1982) 'The demands made on pupils' thinking in mixed-ability classes', in M. Sands and T. Kerry, (eds) *Mixed ability teaching*, Croom Helm, London.

Leahy, S.M. (1988) 'Metacognition and teaching reading comprehension: the effects of strategy awareness training on the question-answering behaviour of students in secondary school', unpublished M.Ed. dissertation, University of Stirling.

Lewis, C.S. (1950) *The lion, the witch and the wardrobe*, Geoffrey Bles, London.
—— (1955) *The magician's nephew*, Bodley Head, London.

Lunzer, E. and Gardner, K. (eds) (1979) *The effective use of reading*, Heinemann Educational, London.

Naughton, B. (1961) 'Seventeen oranges' and 'Spit Nolan' in *The goalkeeper's revenge and other stories*, Harrap, London.

Northcroft, D. (1984) *Hearsay*, Scottish Curriculum Development Service, Edinburgh.

O'Connor, F. (1953) *The stories of Frank O'Connor*, Hamish Hamilton, London.

Peacock, C. (1986) *Teaching writing: a systematic approach*, Croom Helm, London.

Pearson, P.D. and Johnson, D.D. (1978) *Teaching reading comprehension*, Holt, Rinehart and Winston, New York.

Sands, M. and Kerry, T. (eds) (1982) *Mixed ability teaching*, Croom Helm, London.

Scottish Consultative Council on the Curriculum (1989) *Set texts and the context question in Higher English*, Scottish Consultative Council on the Curriculum, Edinburgh.

Seely, J. (1982) *Oxford Secondary English*, Oxford University Press, Oxford.

Tolstoy, L. (translated L. Weiner) (1967) *On education*, University of Chicago Press, Chicago.

Wilde, O. (1978) 'The Canterville ghost', in R.A. Banks (ed.) *Ten ghost stories*, Hodder & Stoughton, London.

Wragg, E.C. (ed.) (1984) *Classroom teaching skills: the research findings of the Teacher Education project*, Croom Helm, London.

Yevtushenko, Y.A. (translated R. Milner-Guland and P. Levi) (1962) *Selected poems*, Penguin Books, Harmondsworth.

Index

51301
203